Dressing Smart in the New Millennium
200 Quick Tips for Great Style

JoAnna Nicholson

Books by JoAnna Nicholson

*Dressing Smart in the New Millennium:
200 Quick Tips for Great Style*

How to Be Sexy Without Looking Sleazy

*110 Mistakes Working Women Make & How to Avoid Them:
Dressing Smart in the '90s*

Color Wonderful

Dressing Smart in the New Millennium
200 Quick Tips for Great Style

JoAnna Nicholson

IMPACT PUBLICATIONS
Manassas Park, Virginia

Dressing Smart in the New Millennium

Library of Congress Cataloging-in-Publication Data

Nicholson, JoAnna
Dressing smart in the new millennium: 200 quick tips for great style/
    JoAnna Nicholson.
    p. cm.

ISBN 1-57023-121-4 (alk. paper)
1. Clothing and dress. 2. Fashion. I. Title.

TT507.N465 1999
646'.34—dc21

99-046636
CIP

Publisher: For information on Impact Publications, including current and forthcoming publications, authors, press kits, bookstore, and submission requirements, visit Impact's Web site: www.impactpublications.com

Publicity/Rights: For information on publicity, author interviews, and subsidiary rights, contact the Public Relations and Marketing Department: Tel. 703/361-7300 or Fax 703/335-9486.

Sales/Distribution: Bookstore sales are handled through Impact's trade distributor: National Book Network, 15200 NBN Way, Blue Ridge Summit, PA 17214, Tel. 1-800-462-6420. All other sales and distribution inquiries should be directed to the publisher: Sales Department, IMPACT PUBLICATIONS, 9104 Manassas Dr., Suite N, Manassas Park, VA 20111-5211, Tel. 703/361-7300, Fax 703/335-9486, or E-mail: dressingsmart@impactpublications.com

Book design by Kristina Ackley

Contents

Chapter
1
Breaking the
Rules

ix

I Am *Very* Grateful to Many *Smart* Women

My Mom,
for encouraging my "developing" sense of style when I was a girl.

My sisters, Jane and Daphne,
for proving that you can look great *everyday* no matter what.

My nieces, Shannon, Randen and Jessy,
for developing their own unique sense of style.

My best friend, Phyllis (she's so amazing),
for her immense on-going support, for her help in editing this book and
for proving that *smart* classic conservative dressers can still be "spicy".

Mary Frances and Allegra,\
for being such special *smart* friends and for their help in editing this
book.

Talitha, the fabulous example for young international style,
for being so *smart* to become both a judge and a fashion designer.

Shu Shu, Jacqueline and Helene, three extraordinary elegant friends,
for being the essence of *smart* international style.

My on-going force of wisdom and clarity—
my beautiful and *smart* confidants:
Phyllis, Shu Shu, Talitha, Mary Frances, Trina, Rusty, Marcia, Audrey,
Dorothy, Chardon, Allison, Sandra, Lil, Wendi, and Lillian.

My exceptional Color 1 Directors of Training for teaching and
coaching new Associates so more women can *Dress Smart:*
Kathleen, Lea, Debbie H., Sachi, Maggie Q., Kate, Marianne, Diane,
Debbie P., and Sylvia.

All of my Associates, including my Directors of Training, for *Dressing
Smart* and showing their clients how to do the same—especially:
Leslie, Ellen Rae, Denise, Elizabeth H., Susan B., Kayo, Rachel, Janet
H-W., Ardith, Judi, Allegra, Elsa, Masami, Beverly, Elizabeth B.,
Yoshiko, Rosemary W., Peggy A., Barbara M., Janna, Keiko, Joanne,
Pauline, Fumi, Susan W., Linda L., Pat, Janie, Marilyn S., Margaret,
Leona, Sue C., Rebecca P., Makiko, Janet T., Marietta, Bonnie E., Usha,

Peggy W., Sandy G., Dorothy, Jeanne S., Carolyn H., Misako, Mary Beth, Sandi, Sherry, Takako, Rosemary L., Lucy, Harumi, Heidi, Kathy, Yuko, Judy, Mimi, Gisel, Jeanne S., Donna, Bonnie G., Mr. Hashimoto, Linda G., Maria Christina, Michiko, Sandy B., Jeannine, Ann W., Sue B., Jan, Rebecca H., Sadako, Barbara B., Joyce, Yolanda, Priscilla, Nancy, Nora, Jane, Ellen, Jan, Suzanne, Mabel Jean, Marlene, Sandy A., Susan H., Ratna, Trish, Robin, Ruth, Evelyn, Ronna, Thelma, Sandra, Lyra, Rebecca A., Marci, Claudine, Yoshi, and Lindsay.

All of my newest Associates for being *smart* to join us and for their desire to share their new knowledge with others:
Maggie, Beth, Deanne, Emily, Karen, Wonder, Jennifer, June, Judy, Pam, and Connie.

I am especially grateful to my publishers, Caryl and Ron Krannich, for believing in me and my life's work.

This book is dedicated to the *awesome Aramis*.

Dressing Smart in the New Millennium

200 Quick Tips for Great Style

JoAnna Nicholson

Special Introduction
By the Publisher

Do you have lots of clothes in your closet, but nothing to wear? Do you look great in pure white, or are you more enhanced by an ivory shade of white? Do you look better in bright shiny pieces of jewelry, or do matte finishes flatter you more? Is your business power look strengthened by the high contrast combination of navy and white paired together, or does that much contrast in your clothing overpower you and diminish your look of authority and competence? Do you always look so great that you would be thrilled to meet your boss, an old flame, or an old school acquaintance whom you haven't seen in years—anytime you step out your door? Or are there days when you go out hoping you won't see anyone you know? Do you know the "rules" for dressing smart, or do you wonder how you missed out on learning such vital lessons.

JoAnna Nicholson knows the "rules" better than anyone. For more than 25 years, she has been a leading force in the image industry, and has helped define and redefine the basic principles of beauty, image, and style. President of Color 1 Associates, Inc., an international image and style consulting firm, JoAnna has trained hundreds of image consultants around the world. A former model, author of four books, and lecturer, her clients include ambassadors, cabinet secretaries, senators, members of Congress, Fortune 500 companies, rock stars, actors, and Miss America. JoAnna and Color 1 have been featured in numerous national and international magazines, including *Glamour, McCall's, Family Circle, Redbook, Cosmopolitan, Money, Architectural Digest, Forbes, Ladies' Home Journal, Harper's Bazaar, GQ,* and *Complete Woman.* Her television and radio appearances include the *Montel Williams Show* and the *Larry King Show.*

The following pages represent one of today's most comprehensive resources for dress and image. Organized as a series of "tips" for success, the book is jam-packed with useful advice on how every woman can look her very best all of the time. Taken together, these 200 tips constitute a crash course in how to dress smart for the new millennium. If you follow JoAnna's advice, you'll avoid many dressing mistakes that can be both costly and embarrassing. Best of all, you'll both look and feel like a million dollars because you've followed JoAnna's simple rule for success—always look your very best.

This is more than just a book and a quick read. Getting advice from JoAnna is like having your own personal trainer and image consultant. She tells it like it is and with a passion shaped by a remarkable career working with thousands of associates and clients on key issues relating to dress and image. If you want to learn more about JoAnna's work, please refer to the dressing smart resource center on pages 228–231. Here we outline numerous resources developed by JoAnna and her associates, including a useful Web site (www.dressingsmart.com), career opportunities, travel adventures, books, and makeup. She also would appreciate your feedback (see the form on page 233) which will be the basis for creating an innovative television program on clothes, makeup, and men hosted by JoAnna.

Author's Introduction

You're About to Begin a Journey That Will *"Change the Way the World Looks at You"*

As you move into the new millennium, you have a mind-boggling variety of clothing, accessory, and makeup styles from which to choose and the freedom to break most of the wardrobing and makeup "rules" of the past. That's great! *Or is it?*

It can be, *IF* you know which rules still stand and *if* you put into practice all of the principles in this book. If you don't, you can be faced with mass confusion and end up looking like you don't have a clue, and/or looking washed-out and ineffective, or garish and over-powered!

You look to fashion magazines for advice and ideas on how to "put yourself together" and find unrealistic pictures of women, most often dressed in clothes you wouldn't wear and/or can't afford. The *smart tips* in this book are arranged in such a way as to help you train your eye to see the differences, **on you personally**, between an unflattering look, a "so-so" look, and a good look and a great look.

Your head-to-toe image can help you land a job or it can cost you a job. It also can have a positive or negative influence on your performance appraisal, your raise, and the recognition you deserve. It may even cause people to overlook you in both your professional and personal lives.

This isn't a gimmicky how to wear the latest fashions book—it's about how to *"look like a million dollars"* **every** day, no matter what your size, age or budget. If this sounds like magic, be assured that it **IS**! But it is magic you can learn to use every day of your life.

1

NEVER Compare, or Judge, Yourself Against the Picture of a Model, a Movie Star, or a Well-Known Woman!

Almost without exception, her picture has been re-touched—probably a dozen times. Our self-esteem and, therefore, our self-confidence, is directly tied to how we feel about the way we look, and our confidence is difficult enough to maintain without comparing ourselves to an impossibly perfect man-made image!

Do you realize what is most often done to a picture before we see it? Even on a 15-year-old dressed like a 30-year-old the "re-toucher" will make her nose look smaller or narrower; move her eyes further apart and make them bigger, more open; add and lengthen eye lashes; reshape eyebrows; erase circles, lines, spots and blemishes; make her lips fuller; clean up her hair line and add highlights. Someone else's eyes can even be "popped-in" digitally! Yikes!! Just imagine what they could do to you or me!!!

2

Compare Yourself ONLY to Whom You are Willing to Become!

You can be attractive no matter your size, age or budget—that's a fact! Six things set one woman apart from another:

- ◆ Knowledge;
- ◆ Self-assurance, self-confidence, self-esteem;
- ◆ A unique sense of style;
- ◆ Attitude;
- ◆ Heart and soul; and
- ◆ "Magic Dust"…you'll find out!

These attributes, gifts, and characteristics have a symbiotic relationship, each taking turns helping, rescuing and strengthening the other. No matter which attribute is strongest at this very moment, all are about to become more powerful and spirited in their support of showing you how attractive you are RIGHT NOW, no matter your age or size, and giving you the gift you've always wanted—that of feeling attractive, intriguing, appealing and stylish. How? *Continue…*

3

Breaking the Rules!

It's the dawn of the new millennium and **FINALLY** we can give ourselves permission to break all of the old rules on how to dress for business and pleasure—except two: **always look great;** and **dress** *smart,* **look** *smart,* **be** *smart!*

Always Look Great!
Whether you are wearing casual, trendy, feminine, classic, vintage, high-fashion, arty, romantic, funky, ethnic, formal, eccentric or workout (in the gym or in the garden) clothes, you will look equally as great!

Did you just think "expensive" when you read "Always look great?" Did you also think, "Now I have to be slim and rich, too?"

Great looking, accomplished women come in all shapes, sizes, and ages. They may be on a tight budget, rich, or somewhere between. They may be shy, outgoing, or both, depending on the circumstances. Although they may spend very little, or a lot, on their clothes they do have one thing in common: they all have developed a great look—they have great style—and they all look elegant! Yes, even in their workout clothes.

Just what does the word *elegant* mean? Lots of things, all good, including:

- Behaving nicely toward others—being gracious;
- Walking gracefully instead of stomping or clomping;
- Sounding elegant—both the tone of your voice and what you say;
- Having a "pulled-together look"—being fashionable, polished and stylish;
- Having charm and clean hair;
- Never making someone feel inelegant or *less*; and
- Dressing and behaving appropriately for the occasion— A CLASS ACT!

You work on being gracious and charming (attitude) and we'll work together on the rest. One thing you will find is that as your self-assurance gets stronger, you will automatically feel and act more charming and gracious.

4

Dress *Smart,* Look *Smart,* Be *Smart!*

Among other things, this means playing by any dress code "rules" your workplace or industry has (written or understood) until you get to the top, at which time **you** get to set the standard.

Create a look for yourself that is even more stunning, yet businesslike, than the code suggests. Look totally "elegant" every day and avoid creating any "visual barrier" that may keep you from reaching your career goals.

Wearing clothing viewed as "appropriate" for your workplace gives the impression that you are highly competent and a team player—it can make you appear to have more knowledge and know-how than others. Be aware!

Dress equal to, or better than, the top female in your company!

Think *quality*, not quantity. Elegant simplicity, not overdone. Never be afraid to wear the same *smart* look often!

Dressing *Smart* also means looking the "part" EVERY DAY, no exceptions! It's what you'll want to do if you want to get a job, keep your job, get a promotion and maybe even meet the man of your dreams!

5

If You Don't Look Great Every Day, It Means That on the Day You Did Look Great it Was an Accident!

Because you don't consistently look great, it shows that you don't know how you did it! It was a fluke! All it takes to consistently look great is:

- Becoming aware;
- Gaining knowledge;
- Training your eye;
- Applying this knowledge and your trained eye to your specific lifestyle;
- The willingness to put your new knowledge into practice every day;
- Maintaining your sense of humor and not forgetting to "play"; and
- Magic Dust...you'll find out!

6

Never Fear Showing Your Best Side

Who made the rule that you need to look *less than fabulous* in order to accomplish your work in an exceptional way? Heaven forbid that you might turn heads when you walk into a meeting—what's this world coming to? Will the meeting accomplish less? I suppose that there are those who feel that it would be better (more businesslike) if you looked forgettable instead of stunning. I would call them nearsighted or, perhaps, jealous.

If more women looked great all of the time, the only "distraction" would be a woman who didn't! Men would be only too happy to get used to women who look fabulous all the time. How do I know? I asked them! If you are fearful that you will look "overdone" and that people will be gazing at you with raised eyebrows instead of admiration, keep your look totally understated, yet elegant. As these *Smart Tips* help you become more accomplished and certain about yourself, you can *go for the gold!*

7

Invest in a Wardrobe that Works for You!

When you shop do you just fatten your closet? Most women really only use about 25% of their wardrobe in any given season. They buy things (lots of them) that they have *never* worn, may never wear, or have worn only once or twice. How many garments do you have that fall into this category? Do some still have the tags on them? Have they been hanging in your closet for several months? Several years?

Let me guess at some of the reasons why something isn't being worn:

- You have nothing to wear it with.
- It was on sale and you just couldn't pass up the bargain even though…
- It doesn't fit, yet.
- You've decided that it's a bad color or that you don't really like it after all.
- It's scratchy!

- It's uncomfortable!
- The right occasion hasn't come along.
- You are saving it.

How would you like to leave the house every morning feeling dynamite about the way you look, never giving it a second thought no matter what you might do that evening and no matter whom you might meet? Learn how to build a *Smart Wardrobe* that works for you—one that you can count on, one that makes you feel *great* every day, one that you love!

8

Wear Boardroom Looks Instead of Backroom Looks!

Throughout years of presenting wardrobe seminars to diverse audiences around the world, I've asked thousands of women to list their **"million dollar looks"**. What's a "million dollar look"? Outfits that, when you wear them, you feel and look like a million dollars.

Without exception, no matter what group—wives of wealthy businessmen and powerful politicians, executive and professional women—*only* two or three women could list anything at all.

STOP BUYING! DON'T BUY ANYTHING AT ALL—**unless it is equal to or better than the best look you have right now!**

Be able to look in the mirror and say, "Yes, I look and feel like a million dollars." If you can't say it, leave it—you will find something perfect the next time you go shopping!

For most women today, money and time are a huge investment and, after all that, if what you buy "sets you back" instead of moves you forward, it doesn't make sense.

You don't have to spend any more money on clothing and accessories than you do now (probably even less) to have "million dollar looks". As a matter of fact, you probably already have a few **FREE $,$$$,$$$** looks hanging in your closet—free, because you don't know they're there!

"Million dollar looks" have nothing to do with how much money you spend on your clothing, they do have everything to do with "investment"—a lifetime investment—because your future will be much brighter based on the way you look right now!

9

Be Careful Not to Get Too Casual— Think Big Picture!

If you are dressed too casually for *your* workplace, you are making a "**visual statement**" that you don't know what's appropriate and/or that you don't care.

Some examples of styles and garments that are too casual looking for some businesses, but appropriate for others, are: jeans and khakis; loafers, sandals and athletic foot wear; T-shirts; and "ski" or other casual sweaters.

While none of these are appropriate in a bank or law firm, each are appropriate in some place of business: an interior designer wearing jeans and a T-shirt with a beautiful jacket; an assistant editor of a sports magazine wearing khakis and loafers; a saleswoman of outdoor clothing or sporting equipment in a ski sweater; a veterinarian in khakis and athletic shoes; and a waitress in a silk tank and matching sarong skirt and sandals serving dinner around a pool.

You are always making "visual statements". No matter where you are going or what you are doing, you are telling people something about yourself. Thinking "big picture" means that to get where you want to be in three years, for example, you may have to pay extra close attention to those visual statements you are making today.

A *"short story"*...
One of my associates, who lives in the same lovely neighborhood as several of her clients, was preparing for a party—she had her hair in curlers and was down on her hands and knees waxing the floor when she ran out of wax. Now, I have to tell you that this is a woman who never has a hair out of place—casual to her means an incredible outfit that many women would wear "out". She doesn't even own jeans and she cooks dinner in a skirt and heels!

Saying a prayer that she wouldn't run into anyone she knew, she covered her curlers with a scarf and ran to the store. Just as she was paying for her wax, this woman came up to her and said, "Aren't you so and so, the image consultant?" She waved her off as she turned to run to her car saying, "No, that's my sister!"

Sloppy equals incompetence!
A sloppy appearance, created by poorly put-together, ill-fitting, unwashed, unironed, mismatched, or stretched-out clothing, sends the message that you don't care how you look and that "you don't have a clue". It makes a loud statement that you are not confident or competent in *at least one* aspect of your life—perhaps casting doubt on your competence in other areas.

10

Defining Style:
Always Read the Small Print

ALL of the *Smart Tips* in this book will help you in developing a stylish look uniquely your own. Each tip you put into practice will bring you closer to training your eye to see what works for you and what doesn't. You'll look in the mirror and be able to say, "My stockings are too light or too dark. I need a different jacket style with this particular trouser shape. My earrings conflict with the buttons on my jacket. My shoes are too heavy looking."

Style—it even "sounds" like a *Smart* word but what does it mean?

It's a word that has a myriad of meanings, all directly related to what you want to achieve.

One connotation is something you strive for, being stylish, as in looking fashionable, chic, contemporary, sophisticated, and pulled-together.

Another has to do with the *shape* or *line* of a garment—there are many "styles" of jackets and trousers. Jacket styles range from feminine and curvy to boxy and classic. Trouser styles vary from narrow to wide legged, from capri to cropped and from pleated to flat front.

Finally, the word can refer to a specific style of dress—western, funky, faddish, trendy, fashion-forward, feminine, menswear, casual, formal, professional/businesslike, sporty, conservative, classic, arty, vintage, or eccentric.

You can even dress in a *different* style every day if you like—having no "set" style is a style of its own. As a young woman, I was told that I should find my own style and stick with it. What I *found* was that I like several different styles, depending on how I feel, where I am going, who I am going with and what I want to accomplish once I get there.

In other words, what image do I want for a specific occasion **AND** what impression do I want to make on others!

It only makes sense, and it's really fun, to dress differently for a meeting with your banker than you do if you are going to a concert **with** the Beach Boys—they were clients of mine. Of course, I dress even differently yet when meeting *potential* future mothers-in-law than when I'm presenting a seminar in Paris at the invitation of the American Embassy, going to a state dinner at the White House in honor of a king and queen, or heading into the jungle to go down the headwaters of the Amazon.

11

Getting Out of the '70s & '80s (and a good part of the '90s) and Into the New Millennium

Wearing clothes, makeup and hair trends, or fads from the past can make you look out of date, out of style, and out of touch! Look great and you *look* as if you know most everything. Look as if you don't have a clue and you'll look like you don't know anything—even if you have a Ph.D.

Can you just "ease" into the new millennium and continue to use things from the past? Even if everything you own is from the '70s and '80s (assuming that it's in good repair and still looks "clean and fresh"), there will probably be some "classic" pieces that you can use and some items that, with a little tailoring, will be fine.

Note that above I used the words "trends" and "fads" from the past. These are usually short-lived fashions (worn from just one season to maybe a couple of years) and those women who continue to *follow* them after they've disappeared from the mainstream *date* themselves—it's like they are in a holding pattern of another era. It may be delightful and endearing when our grandmother or great-aunt looks like she's from another era, but it doesn't "fly" in most arenas today.

There are wonderful classic pieces of clothing like well-cut skirts, trousers, jackets, and tops (blouses, shells, pullovers, crew necks, tanks) that look terrific for years and years—see *Smart Tip #15* for information on how to recognize what's classic and what's not.

There are women who will gracefully glide into the millennium and women who will need to be gently nudged to "get it together"! Some resistance may be natural because, after all, when you are used to seeing yourself the "old (comfortable) way", the "new you" may seem like a stranger you're not sure you can trust.

One client, used to her "ordinary" self, was enticed (actually, I twisted her arm) into purchasing a simple red dress with a small slit on the side. Until she got used to her new stylish image, she would make an amusing comment about herself in the dress looking like "socks on a rooster"! The first time she wore it, a delightful man said, "So, where exactly do those legs end?" She's only 5' 3" tall! **Learn the art of illusion!**

12

The "Mirror Test"...

To start training your eye, learn to do a "mirror test". Place your floor-length mirror where you can walk a few paces away from it—good lighting helps. Study yourself coming and going. Turn around *fast*. If your eye goes immediately to the color or pattern you are wearing it is probably too bright, too bold, and/or too large for you, causing you to look overdone or garish—certainly not a successful look.

If your glance reveals an overall "washed-out" or dull look, the color or pattern is more than likely too muted, too weak, and/or too small for you. Looking drab or mousey is not a radiant, successful look! If your eye goes straight to your belt, necklace, or earrings, for example, they may not be right for you and/or your outfit.

Learn to use your mirror to your advantage and let it help educate you. Check everything:

- Is your shoe too heavy looking? Is the color too light or too dark?
- Is your leg-line being shortened by wearing a longer jacket with wider-leg trousers?
- Does your face look washed-out or overly made up?

- Is your outfit making you look pear shaped—narrower at the shoulder and wider at your hipline?
- Are your colors balanced and coordinated looking? Do they really enhance you?
- Does your hair style make the statement **you** want?
- Do *you* love the way you look?
- Would you be happy about the way you are dressed if you suddenly happen to meet your favorite movie star or the man of your dreams?

13

Dressing *Smart* for Your Industry

How are the top level women in your industry expected to dress—totally classic, conservative, more fashion-forward, trendy, or casual? Once you identify the required look of your work realm, you can plan a wardrobe based on this "expected" attire. Why should you? To disappoint with your image can keep you from moving up. To stray too far from the expected could "get you noticed"—noticed in a positive way or negative way depends on which direction you stray.

Once when I was presenting a wardrobe seminar to the Congressional Wives' Club I had the "nerve" to tell them how extra important it was that they look great every day! No excuses!! Why? Because everywhere they went, they represented **me** and every other American woman!!!

I explained that in this country, women look at them and say, "Oh, that's the wife of Congressman so and so—look at what she's wearing!" When traveling in foreign countries, the women say, (pretend that this is written in French or Italian) "Look, that's Senator so and so's wife, that must be how American women are dressing now."

Whatever you do, I know you want to *look smart* but this is one area where you will want to **think smart**, as well. Play by the rules until you are able to take the lead. Playing by the rules does not mean that I advocate looking dowdy, drab, frowzy, dumpy, or overly conservative just because top women in your field or place of business look this way. I do want you to standout—in the best possible light!

An example: If you work for one of the most conservative firms in a very conservative industry, where no woman has ever worn a pantsuit, I wouldn't advise that you do either. You may wish that "they" would come into the millennium because, after all, women senators and congresswomen are legislating in pantsuits, women journalists are interviewing heads of state while wearing pantsuits—and, the "best" reason so far is that men wear them! *Smile.*

As soon as another woman in the firm ("higher-up" than you) wears the first pantsuit, you can consider the option. Listen for "flack" or any negative comments from **top** leaders. If you think it's safe, "go for it" in the most professional way—wear a beautifully cut pantsuit that is **equal to, or better than, your best suit look!**

If you are in a conservative field like investment banking, you will most likely be dressing in classic attire—*please* don't read boring, mundane, dowdy or uninteresting into the word classic. Classic clothing is never really out of style. How "fashionable" classically styled clothing appears is almost always dependent on the "cut" or "design" of the items and the way you choose to combine them.

For example: Wear a pantsuit that has a very curvy jacket—yes, curvy jackets are classic and at the same time feminine and flattering to all figures. Combine a classic blazer with a just above the knee, *pegged* skirt (it's narrower at the hemline than at the hipline) and you have a much more "fashionable" conservative look than if you paired the same jacket with a "regular"

straight skirt—the difference is a subtle "wow" verses "borrrrrrrrrring."

Regardless of the length of a skirt, have all of your *straight* skirts "pegged". The taper that narrows the skirt starts just below the widest part of your hips and slims gradually to the hem. Very pegged skirts need a kick pleat or a slit so that you can walk gracefully in them rather than "mince" across the room. "Slits" for business attire should not be higher on your leg than the same place a short skirt would end—lower if short skirts are not worn in your place of business.

If your industry is casual, understand really, really well that "casual" and sloppy, stretched-out, faded-out, and worn-out are not synonyms. Dress with a *studied* casualness (think casual elegance) that gives you a well pulled-together look. How? You will know exactly how when you start using these *Smart Tips* and training your eye. More about training your eye in *Smart Tip #24*.

If you work in a field where you may, or are expected to, dress more fashion-forward or trendy, you will be constantly checking-out the latest "must haves" in the fashion magazines and "zany" boutiques. Unless you can afford to, it's best not to buy a lot of the "in" because it's nearly certain to be "out" shortly.

If you are going to "do" one of these looks you'll more than likely need to do it head-to-toe for the look to work. That often requires one or two additional purchases, for example a specific shoe style or bag.

14

Decoding the Terms

Being *fashionable* is always in style but to be considered fashionable one does not need to wear the current looks shown on the runway or in fashion magazines, spend a lot of money, be *thin*, or young.

Actually, even though my field is fashion and beauty, I've become so *anti-fashion* because I'm perturbed (to put it mildly) at the designers for being ridiculous and irked at magazines who continue to show mostly unwearable, unflattering, or unattainable clothing and accessories (from a price standpoint) on undersized models who have been airbrushed a dozen times to bring them closer to so-called perfection. *Yikes*—sorry for the long sentence!

Also, it seems that the "fashion" sections of many magazines have become an arena for photographers to show how "talented and creative" they are by *shooting* leaping, crouching, sleeping, snake wrapped, scary, drugged-out looking women. In many cases, you can't even see what the "model" is wearing and when you can decipher the *fashion*, you usually wouldn't want it anyway.

Years ago, I used to "light-up" when I got the latest issue of any fashion magazine because everything was so beautiful (not affordable, but wearable) and I could get ideas that helped me in my personal quest to be and stay stylish. Now, there is rarely a picture of anything I might want and, for the most part, "lessons" designed to help you be stylish are filled with **really bad advice** or old myths.

15

Classics:
Enduring, Reliable, and Elegant—the Art of Being Timeless, Yet So Current...

Classic styles have perennial appeal, a long life expectancy and they are used every day in some way by most of us. Classics look "stylish" for decades, depending on the ways in which you combine them with each other or with newer "fashions".

Please note that *classic* and *boring* are not synonyms. Classic makeup looks include using lip and blush colors that are always flattering to your coloring instead of following trends like brownish lipstick and blush. Classic ways to wear your hair do not include a lot of teasing or globs of hair spray (helmet hair).

It's almost easier to describe what isn't classic than to tell you what is:

- Anything oversized, overstated or extreme (like big collars and oversized lapels);
- Shoes and boots with platform soles over ¼";
- Very short skirts;
- Very wide pants;
- Sleeves that come down to your knuckles;
- Shoes and boots with very chunky heels;
- Glitz in the daytime;
- Large shoulder pads;
- Brown lipsticks and blush;
- Odd colors of nail polish like purple, green, black, and blue;
- Long, square fingernails and embellished nails;
- Shoes and boots with very square or very pointed toes; and
- Above the knee and thigh-high boots.

Sometimes something is considered classic in a certain region of our country but not in another. For example, in parts of the west and southwest western attire is classic but not in New York City (except jeans, which are classic everywhere). Big hair may be classic in Texas but not in San Francisco.

Wearing "wearable art" is classic for women who have adopted it as their style, and it's a *fashion* for the rest of us. Funky is a wonderfully broad term that seems to be classic for some teens and, depending on the item, a fad or fashion for the rest of us.

16

Fashion-Forward to the New "Silhouettes"

Many of us also wear styles that are currently in-fashion. The "fashions" of today may have started as a fad or trend. And some of these "fashions ala mode" may stay around for several years, if they are worthy of our incorporating them into our wardrobes. They help keep us *contemporary* looking—their life expectancy is "medium" (which is longer than a fad but shorter than a classic). Some "fashions" may actually stay around so long that they eventually are considered classic.

A fashion is most often everything that "falls in the cracks" between classic and fad. Stirrup pants are classic only for skiing and horseback riding. For regular wear, they became a fad and stayed around long enough to become "in-fashion", and then went out of fashion. We liked them because they helped us create a slim hip, broader shoulder look and we wore them with long sweaters and didn't have to worry if our tummies were flat at the moment.

Most of us replaced them with leggings—we didn't need the "stretch pant" look to get the effect we desired. Now, for most out of the house looks, replacing leggings with very narrow-cut trousers made out of one of the micro fibers is the *smart* thing to do.

17

Fast Forward Fads and Trends Definitely Make a Statement—But Is It a *Smart* Statement for You to Make?

The words fad and trend may, or may not, be considered synonyms—it can depend on which magazine you are reading, and it can depend on which fad or trend you are talking about. Nevertheless, they usually have a shorter life expectancy and a smaller "following" than an item that is *in-fashion.*

Fads are usually considered pretty "wild" or "far-out" by current standards. However, they, too, may stand the test of time, become a *fashion* and maybe even a *classic.* Today's fad of hugely thick soles and clunky heels will go the way of the headband of the late '70s/early '80s (the one that went around your forehead, not the *classic* headband that goes over your head).

Although a trend and fad are sometimes the same thing, a trend has another definition that fad doesn't have. For example, pantsuits have become *classic* but wearing pantsuits to work started as a "trend" that has continued to grow—it is not a fad but a viable option for women in almost every work place, no matter how formal or conservative. I am talking about a pantsuit that is **equal** in quality and styling to your skirted suits—not just pants and a top. A tie worn with a pantsuit was a "fad".

Trends are usually more *popular* than fads—more people will try them because although they are a "stretch" for many women, they are usually less of a stretch than a fad!

18
Making Each Purchase Count

Before you invest in any garment or accessory, ask yourself if it will serve you well in your workplace, your lifestyle and help you create the exact look you want. If the answer is yes, and the item is "trendy", ask yourself another question: Are you willing to spend your money on something that you may not be able to wear more than one season? Put another way, are you willing to wear it many times in one season? Do you look and feel like "a million dollars"?

Buy *Smart Basics*

If you're on a budget and want every purchase to count, buy *Smart Basics*. Besides being "classic" in styling what makes a garment a *Smart Basic*? All of the following:

- It's a solid color.
- All stitching matches the garment exactly.
- The color of the buttons match the garment exactly.
- There are no extra details on the garment like epaulets or contrasting trim or braid.
- Its fabric can be combined with many other fabrics.
- It can be worn with many different things.
- Nothing is oversized like collars, etc.
- It's perfectly plain and simple—do not read boring.

19

Don't Sacrifice Comfort for Looks or Looks for Comfort!

You can have both style and comfort if you practice *Smart Tips* and a little restraint.

Almost every day in your place of work, someone, maybe you, has sacrificed comfort for style—particularly in shoes—lovely to look at but uncomfortable to wear. They were so pretty, on sale, too; you just couldn't live without them. Skirts and trousers that are "just a touch" tight in the waist can annoy you all day as can bras that dig into your skin and trousers that are too high in the rise. Have you ever noticed that if you gain weight your pants get shorter? Clothing and accessories that annoy or hurt start getting left at home, making you feel guilty because you wasted your money on them.

On the other hand, **comfort, grubby, baggy and sloppy are not synonyms.** Comfort can be found in any style and shape so it's never necessary to make this sacrifice. When you try something on, sit in it, walk around in it, and ask yourself how it feels on your body. Confining? Scratchy? Uncomfortably tight when you sit? Will you happily reach for it all of the time? Is one size larger the answer?

Follow the *Smart Tip*—don't buy it unless it is **equal to, or more comfortable than the best look you have right now!** And, carefully remove all scratchy tags before you wear something for the first time. If you don't, you may be tempted to "rip it out" in the middle of the day; or the annoyance factor can *contaminate* the way you feel about the item, keeping you from wanting to wear it again!

20

Buy Quality Instead of Quantity!

If you're in it, get out of the habit of buying quantity instead of quality! If you truly want to continually upgrade your look you'll want to always apply this *Smart Tip*, **"If it isn't equal to or better than the best look you have right now, leave it."** When you shop you won't be just fattening your closet. It is far better to wear the same great looking outfit once or twice a week than wear something that looks "so-so" on you!

Why? First of all, **why spend money on something you don't look great in?** You can't afford to look great one day and not the next! It can give the impression that you don't know what you're doing. People who can be consistently counted on are the ones who are promoted—your visual presentation is often even more valued than your work presentations. It doesn't sound fair, but that's the way it often works.

21

Invest in the Right Places!

Spend the most money on the clothes you spend the most time in. This is like learning to "budget" for your lifestyle. Here's a helpful exercise: Write down all of your weekly activities and assign an approximate percentage to them based on the amount of total time you spend doing any given activity—you can make this very clear by dividing a circle into wedges that represent each activity. Your circle will end up looking like an unevenly sliced pie. Wedges might represent work, church/synagogue, sports, family activities, hobbies, dressy evening events, and any other specialized activities.

To help you get started, there are 168 hours in a week. If you sleep 8 hours a night (in a "perfect world"), make a wedge that represents 56 hours (approximately 1/3 of your pie). If you work 8 hours a day and it takes you 30 minutes to drive to work and back, make a wedge that represents 45 hours (this wedge will be a bit smaller than your sleep wedge). Continue making your wedges for each activity—keep in mind that more than one wedge may require the same type of clothing.

When you look at your percentages (or even just the size of your wedges), you'll have a good idea *where* to spend most of your clothing budget. Do you have a clothing budget? Do you even know how much money you spend on clothes each year? Don't most women automatically spend the most money for clothes they wear the most? Some do but others don't. Some women spend a lot of money buying anything that's ON SALE whether they need it or not because they can't pass up a bargain. **It's NOT a bargain if it doesn't look like "a million dollars" on you!**

22

Then There are Other Women Who Buy "Hope"...

The hope of going out to more special dressy occasions (long dresses, cocktail dresses, bejeweled pantsuits); the hope of going away for special weekends and vacations (resort wear, ski wear, cruise wear); the hope of having a special fellow to entertain (you know what goes here); and so on. There is even a magazine ad that says, "In the dress of your dreams, all things become possible."

It's always wonderful to have some "hope" and some "just-in-case" in your closet, but not too much! I once helped a friend buy hope—it was a beautiful, cream colored, silk pantsuit with a romantic, ruffled collar. When she saw it, she said, "This is exactly what I want to wear if Mr. Right asks me to go away with him for the weekend."

"Mr. Right" never did. She *saved* it. It doesn't fit anymore. We still refer to it as buying "hope" and although we've had lots of giggles over it, one can't afford to do this too many times unless one has an unlimited budget. Some ensembles never have a "coming-out party"—it can be sort of sad to see too much hope hanging-out in your closet just waiting for a special "moment" to come or for that "special someone" to call.

My wish for you is that you go through your life collecting many, many special moments. You'll always have something "just right" to wear if you collect only "million dollar looks" **equal to or better than the best look you have right now.**

23

Do You Perceive Yourself Differently Than Others Do?

It's very difficult to look at yourself objectively—it's almost as if you have become immune to yourself. If you feel that:

- Your 10-year-old favorite lipstick and hair style still look great;

- The same style clothing you've gravitated to for eons still looks contemporary on you;

- You don't receive compliments on a regular basis; and/or

- You lament that you continue to attract the same type of men—those who you'd rather not—**it's definitely time to change your image!**

In the mind of another person, you are what he/she thinks you are. The idea is to have the image you want "match" the image you create and have that "match" the image, or message, that's received. Sorry for the convoluted sentence. I'll give it another try.

You want a "Wow!" image. You go shopping and you buy what you think is a "Wow!" look. You wear it to work because you want the handsome new guy to think you look fantastic. The new guy looks at you and thinks, "Nothing." Why didn't he get the message? If you think you are sending one message and a different one is being received, either you aren't on the same wave length (he wouldn't notice you no matter what) or you aren't sending the message you think you are.

Eons ago, when women still wore hats, I was riding up an escalator in a department store—a woman on the down escalator said, "Miss! Miss! How much is your hat?" It took me a moment to realize that she thought I was "modeling" and that my hat was for sale.

I wasn't modeling, BUT I **wanted** to look like a model every waking moment. So, the look that I had created was perfect because the message sent matched the message received.

How did I know how to look like a model? Lessons, practice, and *magic dust* (you'll find out). Truthfully, I was a model; I just wasn't modeling that day.

When you want to "check-out" or change the message you send—your image/your look—your friends and family may not be your best resource for objectivity because they are *used* to you. Change can be unnerving because the "old" you has a certain familiarity and comfortableness. As you begin to look "different" (read: more attractive), heads turn. When you first realize that someone turned to look at you, you may wonder if your slip is showing!

24

A Full-Length Mirror—Not Diamonds— Is a "Girl's" Best Friend

Looking as if you don't have a clue is only caused by not knowing how to use a full-length mirror to your advantage and by a lack of knowledge!

Nothing that reading and applying these *200 Smart Tips* can't fix!

No one can dress well without "training" or without a full-length mirror! Think about training for a minute and about how you would perform in your job if you hadn't been trained to do it. *Dressing smart* is the same principle. Just because you are born *female* doesn't mean that you should be able to dress yourself, your children, and sometimes, your husband, without training.

For example, every woman can type. Yes, you can. Those of you who took lessons type faster and more accurately than those of you who haven't had lessons—without lessons, you can still type but this is called the "hunt and peck" method. With your wardrobe, I call it "hit and miss".

If you've had lessons, do you remember your first typing test? I think that I typed 17 words a minute and made five mistakes. By my second test, I was up to 35 words a minute with three mistakes. *Eventually*, with practice, 80 words a minute, nearly perfect! After lessons, if typing is part of your life, you just get better and better at it.

But, if you stop typing, you can get "rusty"! Besides, new *equipment* is constantly being developed and you may not know how to use it skillfully at first—new styles of shoes, pants in all widths and lengths, skirts in all shapes and lengths, textured stockings, and belts that would have dazzled Cinderella! Consider this book your *magic* lessons for having great style and practice, practice, practice!

How does the full-length mirror help in your training? It helps you train your eye! To train your eye, you must look carefully at yourself, **OFTEN**, and do the "mirror test" whenever necessary. A woman can look at herself in a mirror and say, "I look fine", when she really doesn't (perhaps her stockings are too dark for her ensemble but she can't see this). This woman knows *less* than the woman who looks in the mirror and says, "Something is wrong but I don't know what."

Your knowledge is greater when you can tell what's wrong—"My stockings are too dark." And greater even yet when you know how to "fix" the problem—"I need to change to lighter stockings, perhaps a sheerer version of the same color."

25

Letting Go of Limitations, Bad Advice, and Old Myths

You can create any look, and wear any style you wish, as long as you get the scale, fit, and balance right for your size and shape!

YES, YOU CAN!! You only need *lessons (Smart Tips), patience, perseverance, and your sense of humor!!!*

If your size and/or shape have been a limitation to you in the past, it's only been because your head has been filled with less than accurate advice and a mind set of old myths. A woman needs confidence and knowledge to challenge myths and years of bad advice. If you are full-figured, have full-figured body parts, or you are short, your life has probably been filled with so many DON'TS that you've had very few DO'S to work with—a vast injustice, because you can "DO" everything everyone else can!

All bodies are right—only clothes are wrong!

One of my friends has a **great** looking derriere—her husband speaks of it as her "booty"! She doesn't always need to cover it, she just makes sure that it always looks super. We both love "wild" jeans and some of our jeans have lycra or spandex in them and they are cut quite close in the upper leg. With some of them, she does cover her "booty" with a jacket because they tend to push her derriere "up and out", making it look like a lollipop (her words)! Always check the "view" you are giving others of your back side.

Both very short women and very tall women can look great in long jackets and short jackets, long skirts and short skirts, etc. as can very thin women and very full-figured women. It's all in knowing which particular shapes to combine for your particular shape.

26

Let's Talk About the "Issue" of Weight and Get it Over With!

Most women would prefer to be smaller! Most women postpone feeling attractive until they get small!! Most women never get small or believe they are small enough!!! Most women never *feel* attractive!!!!

This breaks my heart! You have no idea how *really* attractive and stylish you are, or can be, at the exact weight and size you are *right now*! I have proof! Fabulous, non-skinny women include: Kirstie Alley, Queen Latifah, Emme, Kathy Najimy, Oprah, Lisa Nicole Carson, Camryn Manheim, Star Jones, Rosie O'Donnell, Kathy Bates, Delta Burke, Cybill Shepherd, and my sisters, whom I adore.

My *much* older sister (she's really only 16 months older than I) decided a long time ago that even if she wasn't the same size she used to be (before her first child), she is still pretty, she is still sexy, and she isn't going to put-off having fun, really living life! She is fabulous! You can ask her significant other or her boy friends—you can even ask her ex.

What size is she? Well, when she decided that she wasn't going to postpone feeling attractive, she was about four sizes larger than she used to be. She is now the same size as most American women.

My *little* sister (she's barely 5' tall and I'm 5' 8½") has the challenge of being a full-figured petite. Yet, when the company where she works needed someone to teach wardrobing classes to their employees, they asked her to be the instructor.

Why? Because she's the one who has developed a great stylish look—women follow her around and ask her advice. Is she sexy? Men leap out of their 4x4s (she lives in the northwest) when they see her, just to talk for a few minutes—they even stop by work when they don't have any business to do! Well, maybe monkey business.

Now you are suspicious that I don't know what full-figured means. Without giving you her exact dress/suit size, when they asked her to teach the class, I'll just tell you that it was the fourth or fifth size up from the smallest in the plus-size department. Currently she's the smallest size in the same department.

You may still be thinking that you'd rather be smaller than you are, but wouldn't you also like to feel pretty and sexy *right* now? If you've been hiding your body (or your "booty"), or wish you could, you've probably been denying yourself full love of self and life. Many women put their lives into a "holding pattern" until they are a smaller size—you can look terrific now, so why wait? Unrestricted joy of life, and zest *for* life, is possible only if you love yourself, and your body, **NOW**! From now on, instead of "spending" energy and "wasting wishes", just focus on looking great everyday!

27

The Myth About Black

Speaking of myths, did you know that when a woman wears black she almost always looks larger, not smaller? It's true!

Are the colors of the walls in your home and your workplace light or dark? They are usually a light color, right? If you are wearing a dark color and you are standing in front of a light-colored background your body is totally outlined—the reverse of camouflage, it "stands-out"! When you wear lighter colors in front of a light background, you blend in.

Can you at least still wear black at night and look smaller? Yes, If you'll stay outside or sit in a dark chair. So much for that myth! What I **really** think is that you should stop thinking about looking "smaller" and just focus on looking great everyday! If black looks wonderful on you, wear it!

In reality, no matter what you look like, you may do everything all other women can do—you may choose your own "exceptions"—there are always a few. For example, most women with legs that are heavier than they wish won't be wearing **very** short skirts, but they may choose to wear short skirts. Think about it for a second. If only women with perfect legs wore short skirts, very few short skirts would ever be worn!

28

The All Important "V" Shape

For everyone, the best way to get a great stylish look is to create a "V" shape each time you get dressed. It will give you a flattering slimmer-hip, broader shoulder look. You create this "V" shape by making sure that your hipline *looks* narrower than your shoulderline. All you have to do to check this out is to look in the mirror—remember, you are training your eye.

First, take a close look at yourself just in your underlovelies. Some of you will find that your natural shoulderline is wider than your hips and others of you will find that your shoulderline looks narrower (or about the same). If your shoulders look narrower, all you have to do is to make sure that each of your outfits makes your shoulderline look a little wider, most often by using shoulder pads in your tops and/or jackets. **Don't panic**, I don't mean large, football-player pads!

Shoulder pads are great "balancers" for your hips, and for full upper arms, and they can instantly (if situated correctly) create a "V" shape. The opposite of a "V" shape is a pear shape (an upside-down V) which can instantly make a person look dowdy.

What do your upper-arms have to do with your shoulderline? The widest place on your upper-body may be across your upper-arms—you may actually be wider here than at your shoulderline. If you are, you will want to make certain that your shoulder pads are placed far enough out so that the end of the pad is as far out as the fullest part of your arm.

Did you think that women had given up their shoulder pads? Not until men do—they give them the same flattering "V" shape they give us. Most jackets, many blouses, and some sweaters come with padding—most have just gotten smaller.

If your natural shoulderline is at least a touch wider than your hips, you can do without pads in *some* garments. Those garments that make your shoulders look sloped or narrow in comparison to your hipline will still need a little padding.

Placement is critical!

Be aware that many blouses, some sweaters, and some jackets come with the pads situated too close to the neck—simply move them out further. Pin them in place first and take a look in the mirror before you sew them in. Feel awkward around sewing needles? Your cleaners or your best friend will help you.

Speaking of placement, I no longer "assume" that anyone knows which end of a shoulder pad aims which way. A client that had gone from frazzled and frumpy (her words) to so elegant that she was mistaken for the mistress of a wealthy European businessman at a conference they were both attending, was excitedly relating the story when I realized that she had her shoulder pads in backwards. Without interrupting this fun, I simply reached inside the shoulder of her knit top and switched them around.

Did I need to explain what I had done? No. She was, after all, the president of her own company. She just smiled and I knew she would never put them in that way again.

I will, however, explain to you that the thickest part of the pad goes toward the outside edge of your shoulder and the thinnest part goes toward your neck—just in case you don't know.

What was this client wearing the first time everyone at the conference got together? She had told me that she needed something for a cocktail party and dressy dinner the evening before the conference started but her budget and lifestyle did not support the purchase of attire that would be strictly for cocktails. I suggested that she could wear something that we had already added to her wardrobe, an off-white wool gabardine suit.

At my suggestion, she wore it with her matching silk jewel neck blouse, matching very sheer stockings, matching low-cut "pumps" (a pump to her is a 1½" heel), and a matching bag and pearls. Yes, she wore off-white head-to-toe and she looked phenomenal—so can all of you!

More is not better! Besides paying attention to the size of shoulder pads, you need to watch the "layering" of pads—all you need is one but you *might* be able to handle two that are very small. If you place a jacket with pads on top of a blouse with pads, you often have one too many (football, anyone?). If you place a coat with pads on top of your jacket, you probably have two too many!

What to do? If you always work with your jacket on, you won't need shoulder pads in your tops. If you always, or sometimes, take it off, your tops may need padding (keep the pad very "thin") and your jacket padding may need to be scaled down. Since you usually wear your coats over something with a padded shoulder, consider removing the padding from your coats or scaling it way down.

Too large, or too many, pads can make your head look really small in comparison to the rest of your body—it can also make your neck look scrawny. Full-figured petites need to be especially aware of this, as do those of you who wear your hair very short or pulled tightly back.

Other ways to help you create a "V" shape:

- Wear straight skirts that are pegged.
- Avoid A-line skirts—they are an upside-down "V" shape (exceptions are very short A-lines and sometimes A-lines coupled with a jacket that gives the illusion of a small waist and broad shoulders).
- Wear curvy jacket styles that give you a small waist/broader shoulder look.
- Wear trousers that are cut narrow in the leg.

- ◆ Wear tapered-leg trousers (they get narrower as they leave the upper leg and head toward the ankle).

- ◆ If you are going to wear a boxy style jacket or a classic cut blazer, pair it with a pegged skirt or narrow or tapered leg trousers.

29

The Vast Importance of Tailoring

Fit is *so* important to having great style! Expensive garments will look less expensive if they fit poorly, and less expensive garments can look *very* expensive (if the fabric is good) when they are tailored to fit you.

Develop a good relationship with a skilled tailor/ dressmaker and spend the extra money to get the fit right. If you are into quality instead of quantity, you will probably be able to afford this extra expense. If not, **never ever** buy anything that doesn't fit right to begin with! You'll regret it with the first wearing and you'll hesitate wearing it again because you won't "feel" confident when you do.

"Things" to tailor, when necessary, include:

- ◆ Sleeve length,

- ◆ Trouser length,

- ◆ Skirt length,

- ◆ Shape and general fit of jacket,

- ◆ Skirts pegged,

- ◆ Trousers narrowed,

- ◆ Placement of shoulder pads—remove, scale down or add, and

- ◆ Buttons moved.

If a garment is too tight, especially across your bust line or your derriere, it won't look elegant. You must judge, or ask an elegant friend to help you judge, if you simply look stylish and feminine (and maybe just a touch sexy), or too sexy for your workplace. Anything too tight is appropriate for only one occasion—a private party of two!

Jackets that fit too tightly across your derriere are such a prevalent mistake that they deserve their own *Smart Tip*. Make sure that the buttons aren't "pulling" in the front and check the view of your backside, as well.

For a little extra ease, move your buttons over if you can, or ask your tailor if they can let out the jacket. If you can't get any extra room, wear the jacket open—only if it looks good that way. In the front, it should hang as "vertically" straight as possible. If it hangs open in an upside down "V" shape, don't wear it because it will make you look pear-shaped.

Clothes that fit too tight can make you look like you just gained several pounds even if you've just lost 10—they actually make you look bigger instead of smaller.

A jacket that is too big in the hips (sometimes referred to as having too much fabric in the "skirt" of the jacket) can create a frumpy look. I keep wishing that I could come up with different words than "dowdy" and "frumpy", but I haven't. You have to admit that they are pretty descriptive! Sometimes a jacket looks as if it fits perfectly from a front view but from a side view you'll see too much fullness in the back. It's easy to remedy—*please* **have it done, it will make all the difference in the world between your looking ordinary and looking extraordinary!**

The *poor urchin* look of too long sleeves gives the impression that you are wearing "hand-me-downs", your hands are cold, or that you do not know what size you wear. Do you need a petite size only in blouses and jackets? Sleeves with ruffles that are "supposed to" hang down over your hand are fine if they go with your total look, and if you assure me that you won't ask your company for disability if they get caught in a machine. Have too long sleeves shortened, push them up, or roll them up.

You can also push up, roll-up, or let down sleeves that are too short. Sometimes you can get the sleeve length you need by buying blouses and jackets a size (or sometimes even two) larger than you would normally need and then have the body taken in. If you do this, make certain the shoulder still fits properly because that's nearly impossible to change without remaking the entire garment.

30
Avoid Looking Dowdy at All Cost

Looking dowdy or frumpy is caused purely by lack of knowledge and no woman should ever have "that" thought about herself or have anyone else think "that" about her.

Women who look less stylish in the millennium are likely to be viewed as behind the times, out of the loop—not a positive business or social image. All it takes is *Smart Tips*, practice, and *magic dust* (you'll find out).

First, the good news! Dowdy is not a disease, although at times it seems to have reached epidemic proportions in parts of our country and has currently infected the footwear of many women!

Looking stylish instead of frumpy is simply a matter of how you combine clothing items for **you**, how they fit you and how you choose to accessorize them. It's usually a "line-and-design" issue. What in the world is that?

Creating *illusion...*

The eye goes where the line leads it—certain designs or styles can make you appear "squashed" or they can create a "down-line" where you need an up-line (like the up-side-down "V" shape we've been discussing). If the line and design (the shape) of a garment, or the pairing of garments, can create an unflattering look, then the line and design of a garment, or the pairing of garments, can create a flattering look. When you learn how to use line and design to your advantage, you are learning how to create an *illusion*!

Among other things, line and design is:

- The shape of the earrings you choose to wear with your particular shaped face and with your outfit.

- The "placement" of your eye makeup and blush.

- The neckline you choose for your face shape (and, very importantly, your neck size and length).

- Necklines you choose to wear together (a blouse or top with a different neckline than your jacket).

- The shape and length of the jacket (or top) you choose to wear with a particular skirt shape and length, or trouser shape and length.

- The style and weight of your shoe with a particular skirt length or trouser style and length.

- The color and weight (sheer to opaque) of the stockings you choose to wear with any given ensemble. And

- Other accessories, like belts and bags, come into play as well.

31

Smart Line and Design

- To create a longer leg line match shoes, stockings, and trouser or skirt.

- A short jacket (or tucking in your top) creates a longer leg line than a long jacket.

- You can create a longer leg line with a long jacket by pairing it with a straight pegged skirt or narrow trousers—wearing heels helps, too!

- Avoid having too many horizontal lines in one outfit—it's way too *busy*. Starting at the bottom, picture this: the top of boots or shoes next to contrasting opaque stockings, that's next to the hem of a skirt, topped with a contrasting top (worn out over the skirt) ringed with a contrasting belt, and all that topped with a jacket. That's five horizontal lines!

- Tunics and tops, overall, need to end *just barely* at the bottom of your derriere, otherwise they make your legs look short! Most of the tops in the plus-size departments (and maternity shops) are way too long—do a "mirror test" and shorten tops when necessary.

- If you have a short waist (it may seem like it starts right under your bosom) wear skirts and trousers that do not have a waistband or have a very narrow band. (From this point on, I will often be referring to skirts and trousers as "bottoms", and blouses, tanks, shells, pullovers etc. as "tops".) If you are short-waisted, "fool" the eye into believing otherwise by: wearing tops and bottoms that match (this is called a base); "blousing" your tops (pulling them out a little); wearing your tops out; or by matching a belt (that rides down on your hips a bit) to the color of your top.

- Having a long waist (lots of space between your bosom and waist) is generally not a concern but if you would like it to appear higher, you can wear skirts and trousers with wider waist bands or belts that "ring" the waist in the same color as your bottom.

- If you have a very pointed chin you wish was a different shape, you may want to avoid V-necks—or, you may decide to love the unique beauty of your chin.

- For eons, women with round faces have been counseled to wear V-necks to make their faces appear less round. First of all, round faces are beautiful and exotic, just as are broad square faces and any other shaped face—and line and design is complex! Let's just say that you do want to "lengthen" your round face, so you wear a V-neck. If your round face is attached to a long thin neck, you have just made your neck look longer and thinner— for good line and design, everything has to be considered!

- Don't forget, if you have narrow or sloping shoulders or are wearing a top that gives you that look, wear shoulder pads.

- If you have a long torso (or a long waist), avoid trousers and skirts that hang down on your hips—if you like, you can make this look work by wearing a top that matches your bottom or wearing your top out instead of tucking it in.

- Avoid all dirndl style skirts and A-lines (a short A-line is the exception), as their shape— an upside down "V"—can make you look dowdy.

- Knits and other "soft-wear" fabrics that drape easily are great for all body types.

- Hair that is tightly pulled back could be making your body look bigger than it is—look in the mirror to check for good balance.

- A defined waistline makes any bosom appear more ample.

- Pleated trousers are great for all body types as long as they fit correctly—no spreading pleats or pockets.

- Shoes with a high vamp make your legs look shorter; those with a low vamp lengthen them (a low vamp is when the top of the shoe is cut so that you can *almost* see the beginning of your toes—a very low-cut vamp would show a little "toe cleavage").

- Shoes with thick heels can make full calves look larger and thin calves look like toothpicks.

- Be aware that single button jackets, intended to button at the waist, may button either too high or too low on you. Too low can make your legs look short, too high can cause your legs to look as if they start right under your bosom. Check this on all of your jackets, no matter how many buttons they have.

- If you feel your body looks better nude than clothed, you aren't wearing the right clothes.

- If you have broad shoulders, give thanks!

32

Color—It's the Most Important "Accessory" and It's Free

Why am I calling color an accessory? Because it is an *adornment*. If you just know how to work with color for *your coloring*, you will look more phenomenal, by far, than you can without this knowledge. Edith Head, the famous Hollywood costume designer, referred to color as a *powerful tool* that should be used as a precision instrument to bring out a woman's beauty.

Let me tell you right now that I do not believe in any of the seasonal or cool/warm color theories. The following *Smart Tips* are what I *do* believe:

Approximately 50% of you look stunning in bright, clear, vibrant colors. The other half of you look most stunning in colors that have less brightness—those that are more subdued or muted looking. How can you tell which "clarity" is best for you?

The magic of clarity! What *does* that word mean, anyway?

Clarity has to do with the amount of "brightness", or lack of brightness, of a color—how "clear" or "toned-down" the color appears. *ALL* colors come in different clarities. There are:

- Bright, "bold", vibrant, clear reds, like a fire engine, for example.
- Bright (but not so bold) more "delicate" looking clear reds like a strawberry.
- Slightly more subdued, more "muted" (less bright and bold) reds like a ruby.
- And even more subdued and muted, toned-down reds like a dusty rose.

If a color is too bright and bold for your coloring, it can look garish, and by comparison, you will look washed-out and overly pale, even sickly. That's a clue that you are one of those women who will be more enhanced by more "delicate" looking brights or by more subdued, muted, toned-down colors.

If, on the other hand, a color is too subdued or toned-down for your coloring, it can gray, muddy, or even sallow your skin, causing you to look drab. That's your clue that you are in the approximately 50% of women who are more enhanced by bright and bold, or bright but "delicate", clear, vibrant colors.

You can experiment in front of a mirror—it's very important to use good light. Hold different clarities up to your face. Some of the best colors to work with are reds, blues, and blue-greens. Start with a comparison of bright colors—one **BOLD** and bright, the other "delicate" and bright. Holding up the boldest, brightest first, just glance at yourself and see if your eye goes right to the color or to your face and the color at the same time.

If you "*hold your own*" and your face looks fresh, radiant and alive, the boldest, brightest colors will look fabulous on you. If your glance brings your eyes immediately to the color, it's too bright and bold for your coloring.

Try a more delicate looking bright color next. If your face "lights-up" and looks clear and radiant, you've found your best clarity! But, if the color still appears to "jump forward" or "jump-off" your skin, and you look washed-out, pale or sickly, you'll know that you need more subdued, toned-down colors to make **YOU** *glow.*

If you compare just slightly toned-down, subdued colors to very toned-down, subdued colors, you will find that you look more radiant in one of these clarities than the other. Watch for your face to "light-up" versus looking dulled or grayed. The right clarity "brightens" your face, making it appear fresh and alive while the wrong clarity instantly dulls your face (like a shadow has been cast upon it), taking away your radiance.

33

For an Extraordinary Appearance, Wear Your Most Flattering "Shade" of Every Color in the Spectrum!

Now that you have an understanding about the importance of clarity we need to work on *shade.* There are many different shades of every color in the spectrum and you'll look extraordinary in your red, for example, but not so "hot" in mine—remember that we are each wearing our reds in our best *clarity!*

Do women instinctively know what colors are flattering to them? Rarely. What most women do when they look in the mirror is to check out everything "from the neck down"—the style and the fit. Because their eye hasn't been trained to see what the color is doing to their skin tone, they seldom comment accurately on the color. Even I was one of those women.

A "short story"...

Once upon a time, a long time ago, I was a "creature" of fashion—I cared about style and the way something looked on my body.

I needed to buy a "perfect" dress, so I did. It was going to be the dress I changed into after my wedding (I think they used to call them going away outfits), and much more importantly, it would be the dress I would be wearing to teas and receptions in "my life to be" as the wife of an Air Force pilot.

How did I know how to pick out a "perfect" dress? I had been a model and had taken fashion and wardrobe classes in college. What did it look like? It was:

◆ Elegant,
◆ Understated,
◆ Classic,
◆ Beige linen (I was headed south),
◆ A wrap style with a shawl collar,
◆ Fitted at the waist, but not tight, and
◆ A mid-knee length.

Truly, over the next two years, it was the perfect dress for many occasions. There was only one problem—I wouldn't wear it! Why? It didn't look good on me but I didn't know why. All I knew was that I loved it but every time I put it on and looked in the mirror, I had to take it off. With all my fashion knowledge, I couldn't figure out what was wrong. When I finally figured it out, it changed my life forever.

It was the wrong "shade" of beige for my skin tone! It made me look totally drab!! Suddenly I knew that the perfect dress (or any other clothing item or accessory) is not perfect unless it is also **color perfect!!!**

Why was this realization so life changing? In exactly the same time frame, I met Judy Lewis-Crum and together we founded Color 1 Associates, our company of International Image and Style Consultants. We were the first firm in the world to train color and image consultants, making us two of the founders of a new industry—an industry that has changed the lives of countless women!

Clients have commented during color charting sessions, as they view for the first time all of the shades of colors that have just been selected just for them, that many of these exact colors represent all of their old *favorite outfits*—the ones they used to love to wear because they always brought so many compliments! Clients who are grandmothers (and even great-grandmothers) are still receiving compliments—when you are in this age group and *young women* are telling you how fabulous you look, you know you are doing it right!

Every one of you can wear at least one **specific shade** of *every color* in the spectrum and look fantastic—on some of you, a few of your "best shades" may need to be combined or "accented" with another to create the right strength or delicateness for you! There are *numerous* different shades of:

- beige,
- camel,
- brown,
- gray,
- green,
- blue-green,
- robins egg blue/teal,
- blue,
- several shades of purple,

- plum/fuchsia,
- raspberry,
- red,
- red-coral,
- coral,
- a pinky orange or orange,
- yellow/gold,
- rust,
- white (all women can wear "white," but not all women can wear pure white),
- navy, and
- black (most, but not all, women are enhanced by black).

I know that some of you have just decided that I'm crazy because I'm telling you that you can wear a certain color that **you're certain** you don't look good in—green, yellow, or brown, perhaps. Actually, if you haven't been wearing these colors I'm glad, because if you don't know exactly which "shade" of each of these you look great in it's easy to make a **MAJOR** mistake.

Of all of the greens, for instance, lime, celery, Kelly, mint, olive, jade, parrot, spring, emerald, sea, forest, apple, moss, sage, grass, etc., there is most often only one that will be wonderful on you. Yellow can be difficult, but when you get it right for you, it's amazing and it can be combined so well with all of your other best colors. Brown may be the most difficult to get right because if you don't get it perfect, it's a disaster as a clothing color. But when it's good, it's very, very good!

Everyone can wear both "cool" and "warm" colors but without seeing you in person, it's difficult to guide you to your very best *shades*. However, as you train your eye to see your best clarity, you will begin to notice how your face either glows (lights-up), or looks sallow, grayed, or muddy—the *right* or *wrong* shades of colors do the same!

Even though I can't see you, I can give you some "colorful" *Smart Tips:*

- The most wearable shades of green have a touch of blue in them (like emerald green) versus the more yellow greens (like lime green).

- Blue-greens, turquoises, robin egg blue and teal are universally flattering colors—don't forget to wear them in your best clarity!

- A shade of blue that is closer to turquoise than it is to blue-purple is more universally enhancing than the "royal" blues.

- Every one of you can wear several shades of purple. Those purples that fall in the "middle" of the purple spectrum are usually more universally flattering than those that fall at each end—the blue purples and the red purples.

- Each of you can wear some shade of raspberry. But, in the case of plum and fuchsia, most of you will find a becoming shade, but be very careful here; the wrong shade can really sallow your skin.

- You all have your best red—your body's natural red color is a deeper tone of the color you naturally blush, the same color as your fingertips and the inside of your lower lip.

- All of you can wear a shade of coral, and you can also wear a shade of "red-coral"—picture a shade that would fall right between your red and your coral.

- "Orange" is available to all of you but the shade of orange that you may be *picturing* is wearable by only a few of you. The most flattering oranges have "pink" in them and they are often very close in shade to your coral.

- Everyone can wear at least one shade of yellow—picture how many different shades of yellow there are and that will help you understand that someplace between buttercup and lemon, there will be a shade of yellow that is perfect for you! Beware of the more brownish golden yellows, like mustard, as they are rarely as flattering.

- What about gold? Not everyone can wear a shade of gold successfully. If you don't look equally as good in a gold as you do in your yellow, avoid it. If you *love* gold and want to wear it anyway, wear it with other enhancing colors or mixed in a print.

34

Smart Tips to Help You Find Your Most Stunning Neutrals!

These tips *assume* that your hair color and hair highlight color are really flattering to your skin tone (not necessarily *natural*, but becoming nevertheless):

- You'll be learning all about your best whites in a few minutes.

- Your best beige matches your skin tone exactly or, if your skin is darker, it is a lighter version of your skin tone.

- If your hair is light, your best camels and browns are a darker version of your hair color and/or your hair highlight color.

- If your hair is medium in tone, your best camels will match your hair color and/or hair highlight color (they could also match your skin tone if it is "camel", or caramel). Your best browns will be a darker version of your hair color and/or your hair highlight color.

- If your hair is brown, your best camel will be a darker version of your skin tone; match your skin tone; if your skin tone is darker, a lighter version of your skin tone; or possibly your hair highlight color. Your best browns will match your hair color and/or hair highlight color.

♦ If your hair is very, very dark brown or black, as explained above, your best camels will either be a darker or lighter version of your skin tone or they will match it exactly. Your best browns will be a darker version of your skin tone or, if your skin tone is darker, they will match it exactly.

♦ Your best gray will not have any brownish or muddy quality to it—blue-grays are more universally enhancing.

♦ Your best rust will not look burgundy, orangish, or brownish on you—it will look "rust".

♦ You may be able to wear several shades of navy but they will all have something in common—they will all be lighter or darker versions of the same "shade" of navy. Avoid shades of navy that sallow or gray your skin.

♦ Black—*Continue...*

35

Ah, Black...

Most of you can wear black and look great—it's *how* you wear it that can make the difference between your looking elegant and looking drab. On some of you black will need:

♦ A touch of color near the face.

♦ More skin showing—lower neck versus turtle neck.

♦ Less black—sheer tint of black stockings with black skirt/dress instead of opaque.

- A touch of *metallic*—jewelry. It could be gold, silver, copper, etc., but those of you who have golden skin tones, or golden, camel, caramel or bronze colored hair, or hair highlights, will want to use gold. If your hair color is red or has red or copper highlights, copper will look phenomenal.

- Black, or black and metallic, earrings or headband—you are "tying" the black into your skin tone and hair colors, creating balance and making it look like there is a *relationship* between your coloring and the black.

- A *delicate* use only, like black lace over a skin toned fabric.

- To be worn only as a small amount in a print combined with your best colors and neutrals, or not at all.

How can you tell which is your most flattering way(s) to wear black? Your "mirror test" will help you figure it out. Experiment with the various ways listed above. If you find that no matter what you do, black looks "out-of-place" or "foreign" on you, don't wear it (except, perhaps, as a small amount in a print).

Don't be disappointed! Knowing once and for all is liberating, and I know that you definitely wouldn't want to show up in black at an interview, or for a party, and compete with other women who look great in it! Pick another neutral that looks fabulous on you and designate it as **your** black! Don't overlook cream— your "black" doesn't have to be a dark color.

36

Do You Look *Smashing* in PURE White or Does it Look *Cheap* on You?

I hate the word "cheap" but I'm using it because, in this instance, it is so descriptive that I know you'll pay extra close attention to what follows!

What am I talking about? As strange as it may seem, only 50% of you are flattered by **pure** white while all of you can wear "clean looking" *soft whites, off-whites,* and *creams.* Use your mirror test.

If pure white tends to "jump off your skin" and look visually too bright or inexpensive (cheap), wear softer whites, off-whites, and creams. Sometimes whites, off-whites, and creams have a brownish "oatmeal" or grayish "putty/taupe" cast—*please* avoid these! And, unless your skin tone is golden, avoid yellowish looking whites, yellowish looking off-whites, and yellowish looking creams.

Some of you have whitened your teeth to the point that they are too white for your coloring—do a mirror test.

37

Creating "Instant" Impact

Wear color combinations that look fabulous on you instead of those that give you a "headless" look or a drab look!

Let's assume that you are wearing your most flattering "shades" of each color in the spectrum in the best "clarity" for you. Can you combine these colors in anyway you like and look great? Sorry, **NO!** You also have "most becoming" color combinations.

A few women have a wonderful sense of style in that they have a knack for creating great looks. Unfortunately, if a woman with this ability doesn't pay attention to *her* best colors, clarity, and color combinations, she may be looking stunning only from the neck down!

Why? Half of you have "strong" coloring and are very flattered by gutsier color combinations for your clothing and makeup. The other half of you have "delicate" coloring and are very enhanced by using delicate color combinations for your makeup and clothing. Once you know your "Color Type" I'll give you the *specifics* on **your** best combinations.

What is a Color Type?

A Color Type is simply a *description* of your coloring (skin tone and natural hair color) and/or a *description* of your best "look" for clothing, makeup, and interior design (yes, I want you to live in space that is enhancing to you—check the Resource Center). For example, I have an ivory skin tone and very dark brown hair—there is a great deal of "contrast" between my skin tone and hair color. Therefore I am a Contrast Color Type and my very best looks for clothing, makeup, and interior design all revolve around my creating **needed** *contrast.* Not all Contrast Color Types have contrast between their skin tone and their hair color (the reason for the "and/or" above). Their skin tones may be medium or dark but they also absolutely **need** the same *contrast* in their clothing and makeup looks—no other look is as fabulous!

Finding your Color Type

The following lists of well-known women with their Color Type, best "clarity" and the designation of "strong" or "delicate" will help you make a decision that will be **LIFE CHANGING!** Why so serious, suddenly? Because, if you want to look your **absolute best** *FOREVER*, nothing is as important!

Although I have made only four lists, there are really **12** different Color Types because MANY people are a cross between two—half delicate coloring and half strong coloring, for example. If this is you, you will find that you walk a fine line between being overpowered and being underpowered! For some of you, a "light" just went on—now you know why it's been so hard for you to get it *right.* Now that you know, your full-length mirror will help keep you on track. More about "Cross Color Types" soon.

How dark or light your skin is has nothing to do with your Color Type—I am referring to all women of all races. The darkest skin tones and lightest skin tones are found in all 12 Color Types; you can't change your color type by changing your hair color.

Also, there are no single categories for all blondes, all brunettes, or all redheads; nor are there for all Black, Asian, Hispanic, Native American, or Caucasian women. There is a huge variety of coloring among all women, whatever race. Black, Asian, Native American, Hispanic, and Caucasian women are found in all 12 Color Types. Black and brown hair are in all 12. Natural blondes in at least six different Color Types (could be more, it depends on what you think of as "blond"). And, redheads in about five (again, depending on what you think of as a "redhead").

Contrast Color Types—Bright, Bold Clear Colors and Strong Coloring

Jacqueline Kennedy, Elizabeth Taylor, Winona Ryder, Toni Braxton, Connie Chung, Cher, Diahann Carroll, Audrey Hepburn, Giselle Hernandez, Queen Elizabeth, Carol Simpson, Demi Moore, Jessica Yu, Rita Moreno, Minnie Driver, Judith Dench, Fran Drescher, Courteney Cox, Lucy Liu, Catherine Zeta-Jones, Joan Collins, Barbara Bush, Lynn Whitfield, Julianna Margulies, Christina Ricci, Monica, Dixie Carter, and Ruth Bader Ginsberg.

Natural hair colors are dark brown or black. Skin tones range from ivory and olive to dark brown.

Light-Bright Color Types—Bright, but Delicate, Clear Colors and Delicate Coloring

Princess Di, Tyra Banks, Jewel, Hillary Clinton, Janet Jackson, Marilyn Monroe, Claudia Schiffer, Sharon Stone, Ce Ce Winans, Faith Ford, Cameron Diaz, Kristi Yamaguchi, Diana Ross, Melanie Griffith, Ivana Trump, Mary Hart, Dolly Parton, Sandra Day O'Connor, Gwyneth Paltrow, Deborah Norville, Charlize Theron, Heather Locklear, Courtney Love, Portia de Rossi, Vivica Fox, Elizabeth Shue, and Diane Sawyer.

Natural hair colors range from golden blond to black (but do not include red). Skin tones range from ivory to dark brown with probable golden tones.

Gentle Color Types—Toned-Down, Subdued Colors and Delicate Coloring

Gwyneth Paltrow, Katie Couric, Annette Benning, Candice Bergen, Beverly Johnson, Calista Flockhart, Jane Leeves, Nicole Kidman, Elizabeth Hurley, Drew Barrymore, Kim Basinger, Meryl Streep, Beverly Johnson, Glenn Close, LeAnn Rimes, Jane Seymour, Jane Pauley, Phylicia Rashad, Michelle Pfeiffer, Betty Ford, Kate Moss, Cicely Tyson, Claire Danes, Jodi Foster, Roma Downey, Cybill Shepherd, Linda Evans, Alek Wek, and Nicole Kidman.

Natural hair colors range from blond to black and include some redheads. Skin tones range from ivory and pink beige to dark brown with probable pink tones.

Muted Color Types—Slightly Toned-Down Colors and Strong Coloring

Cindy Crawford, Oprah, Julia Roberts, Barbara Walters, Jennifer Lopez, Bai Ling, Naomi Campbell, Sophia Loren, Mariah Carey, Kathie Lee Gifford, Salma Hayek, Whitney Houston, Shirley MacLaine, Nancy Reagan, Whoopi Goldberg, Maria Shriver, Daisy Fuentes, Barbra Streisand, Gloria Estafan, Tina Turner, Jennifer Esposito, Geena Davis, Christine Lahti, Patti La Belle, Lauryn Hill, Carmen Electra, Sheryl Crow, and Susan Sarandon.

Natural hair colors range from blond to black and include some redheads. Skin tones range from ivory beige to golden beige and from olive to dark brown.

When your hair turns "gray", silver, or white, your color type **stays** the same. Sun damaged skin, skin rashes/diseases, high doses of some chemicals, and some vitamins *might* change the color of your skin tone and, if permanent, *might* change your Color Type.

Cross Color Types

There are as many Cross Color Types as there are straight Color Types. Here are some *Smart Tips* to help you find yourself:

- Contrast/Muted Color Types might look just like a straight Contrast Color Type but instead of clear colors, they look best in slightly toned-down colors. The natural hair color is very dark brown (with probable reddish highlights) or black.

- Muted/Contrast Color Types, on the other hand, look best in clear colors instead of slightly toned-down colors. They are not straight Contrast Color Types because their color combinations need to look more "muted". The natural hair color is dark brown (with possible reddish highlights) or black.

- Contrast/Light-Bright Color Types may need to *slightly* "take the edge off" their clear bold colors, making them just a hint more delicate looking. The natural hair color is dark brown (with probable golden highlights) or black.

- Light-Bright/Contrast Color Types usually need slightly more powerful color combinations than a straight Light-Bright Color Type. The natural hair color is brown to dark brown (with golden highlights) or black.

- Light-Bright/Gentle Color Types might look like a straight Light-Bright Color Type but they need slightly toned-down colors instead of clear, bright, delicate looking colors. Natural hair colors range from blond to black.

- Gentle/Light-Bright Color Types need clear, delicate looking bright colors instead of a straight Gentle Color Type's toned-down colors. Natural hair colors range from blond to black.

- Gentle/Muted Color Types have half-delicate, half-strong coloring so some of the very
blended small patterns that look ethereal on
a straight Gentle Color Type may look weak,
requiring them to strengthen color combinations when necessary. Natural hair colors
range from blond to black and include some
redheads.

- Muted/Gentle Color Types have half-strong
and half-delicate coloring so some of the
darker or gutsier color combinations that look
so rich on straight Muted Color Types may
look "heavy" or overpowering. Lighten darker
color combinations when necessary. Natural
hair colors range from blond to black and include some redheads.

38

Are "You" the Center of Attention or is Your Outfit?

Yet another *technical* thing to discuss—"high-contrast". Believe me, I wouldn't be writing about it if it
weren't very important! How important? If 50% of
you do "it", you aren't looking your best—to be truth-
ful, you're looking pretty bad!

High-contrast is created by wearing

- Black with white—like a black suit with a
white blouse; a black and white stripe sweater
with black jeans; or a black dress with white
pearls.

- Black with off-white or cream—like a cream
suit with a black necklace and black shoes;
or a black and off-white print blouse with
black trousers.

- Navy with white—like a navy suit with white piping on the jacket; a navy skirt with a white top; or a white suit with a navy T-shirt.

- Navy with off-white or cream—like a navy suit with a navy and cream scarf; or navy shorts with an off-white tank top.

- And sometimes very dark brown with white— like dark brown leather pants with a white sweater.

All three Contrast Color Types who have not changed their hair color to a more muted tone, and all three Light-Bright Color Types look great in high contrast. All three Gentle and all three Muted Color Types are overpowered by these high-contrast color combinations—that means that if you are wearing them and you walk into a room, your outfit will enter ahead of you. They give you a "headless" person look. If your hair is very dark brown, you may be able to handle the contrast between dark brown and white; if not, it's best to avoid it.

Not sure about your Color Type? Your mirror will tell you if you should avoid high-contrast—try it and see where your eye goes. If your eye goes to the color combination before it goes to you, you are one of the Gentle or Muted Color Types. Substitute your best light beige for the white and look at the **spectacular difference**. For you, beige with black or navy creates a slightly softer contrast and a much more stunning entrance!

Which Color Types are enhanced by "pure white"?

- Contrast Color Types can wear pure white head-to-toe.

- Light-Bright Color Types can do the same.

- Gentle Color Types can wear a small amount of pure white in a small print or as a trim.

You can wear soft whites—a white that still "looks" like white on you but isn't so bright-white that it jumps off your skin, off-whites, and creams. Wear them with any color except black, navy, and *probably* dark brown.

♦ Muted Color Types should avoid pure white in any amount. Just like all Color Types, you can wear soft whites (they will still "look" like white on you without being so bright-white that they jump off your skin), off-whites, and creams. Wear them with any color other than black, navy, and *probably* dark brown.

39

Is Your Coloring "Delicate" or BOLD?

If your coloring is *delicate* looking (Light-Bright and Gentle Color Types), you will want to make all of your color combinations delicate looking too. If your coloring is *strong* (all Muted and Contrast Color Types), your color combinations need strength.

"Picture" it. If you have a painting that needs to be framed, you would never pick out a powerful, bold looking frame for a gentle looking watercolor. Nor would you select a delicate looking frame for a bold graphic.

If your *coloring* is "delicate" (this term has nothing to do with your personality), **lighten-up darker colors and dark, or strong, color combinations**—you could also avoid wearing them. For example:

♦ The strong color combination of a navy suit worn with a red blouse can be lightened-up by putting gold buttons on the jacket and wearing gold or navy and gold earrings. But you can also easily solve the dilemma by wearing a pink, yellow, or other light color top, in place of the red.

◆ Could you add just a gold or silver necklace to lighten the dark combination of a forest green sweater and brown trousers? A tiny chain is not enough but a more substantial looking necklace and earrings will help. Adding a brown belt with a buckle in the same metallic will give you even better balance. Or, you can add a scarf that combines the green and brown with some lighter colors.

If your *coloring* is "stronger", "gutsier" looking, it's not necessary for you to lighten strong color combinations but you will probably need to **lighten, strengthen, or brighten** other *specific* color combinations.

As you read the following examples, remember that we are discussing those of you who have STRONG coloring. By the way, you do know by now, that having strong coloring doesn't have anything to do with your personality or body shape and size! Right?

If you are a Contrast Color Type, you will need to add a light or bright accent to an all dark color combination (the exception is black **if** you look great in it head-to-toe), and a bright or dark accent to an all light color combination—you could also avoid wearing them. An example:

A clear light pink top and cream trousers are strengthened by a black belt and black shoes. A dark purple top with a navy suit can be brightened by adding a scarf that combines the navy and purple with white/cream and/or any bright color. Or, you can always just change your top to one that is a bright color or a light color.

If you are a Muted Color Type you will not need to lighten dark color combinations **unless your hair is light**. If your hair is medium to dark in tone, you may need to strengthen light color combinations (add a medium or dark color) or wear them in large blocks of color like a coral skirt with a yellow sweater. Avoid wearing small patterns that combine light colors—they aren't "gutsy" enough for you.

40

Here Are Your Best *Color Combinations* by Color Type

I've given you some "unusual" examples to *stimulate* your imagination—you may substitute "your" favorite neutral, or light, medium, or dark color.

CONTRAST COLOR TYPES

- ◆ Wear a dark color with a bright color—black and red; navy and fuchsia.

- ◆ Wear a bright color with a light color—turquoise and white; purple and pink.

- ◆ Wear two bright colors together—yellow and blue; fuchsia and red-coral (I mentioned that I'd be giving you some "unusual" color combinations—I wear my fuchsia suit with a red-coral top and "tie" it all together with a fuchsia and red-coral scarf).

- ◆ Wear a dark color with a light color—black and white; navy and yellow.

- ◆ Avoid using two light colors together without adding a medium or dark color—cream and light gray with red; white and pink with black.

- ◆ Avoid using two dark colors together without adding a light or medium accent—black and dark purple with white; navy and rust with cream.

LIGHT-BRIGHT COLOR TYPES

- ◆ Wear a light color with a bright color—cream and robins egg blue; red and white.

- Wear two medium toned "delicate" looking bright colors together—yellow and coral; medium pink and purple.

- Wear a dark color with a light color—black and white; charcoal gray and light blue.

- Two pastels worn together, like beige with light purple or light green with light yellow, might need a contrasting accent (a bright or dark color); or wear the light colors in large blocks of color, like a top and bottom versus combined in a small pattern.

- Avoid wearing a bright color with a dark color without adding a light accent—red and black with gold buttons and or gold jewelry.

- Avoid wearing two dark colors together. If you do, you will definitely need to lighten the color combination—dark green and charcoal gray lightened with jewelry, matching metallic buttons and/or a large block of a light color (a white top, perhaps).

GENTLE COLOR TYPES

- Wear two light colors together—pink and yellow; light gray and beige.

- Wear a light color with a medium color—light blue-purple and raspberry; cream and camel.

- Wear two medium colors together—coral and purple; medium gray and camel.

- Wear a medium color with a dark color—medium green and dark green; medium raspberry and navy (light-haired Gentle Color Types will need a light accent near the face or at the waist).

- Avoid wearing the high-contrast combinations of black, navy, or dark brown with white/off-white/cream—substitute your light beige or any other light color.

- Avoid wearing two dark colors together, especially if your hair is light to medium in tone. If you do, you will definitely need to lighten the color combination—dark red and charcoal gray lightened with jewelry, matching metallic buttons and/or a large block of a light color (like a light gray top, perhaps).

MUTED COLOR TYPES

- Wear a light color with a medium color—beige and green; pink and gray.
- Wear two medium colors together—red and camel; medium gray and blue.
- Wear a dark color with a medium color—navy and purple; rust and teal.
- Wear two light colors together in larger blocks of color (coral trousers and yellow top) or accent lighter color combinations with a medium or dark color—light green and beige with rust; cream and light gray with camel.
- Wear two dark colors together (light-haired Muted Color Types will need a light or medium accent)—navy and rust; dark green and brown; dark plum and black.
- Avoid wearing the high-contrast color combination of black, navy and probably dark brown with white/off-white/cream—substitute your light beige or any other light color.

41

Illuminating Your Business World...

Contrary to old notions, all colors and color combinations can be successfully worn in any place of business. If you are wearing a red suit and want it to look more "conservative", wear it with a neutral colored top instead of one in yellow or purple, for example, which are more avant-garde color combinations.

On the other hand, if you have conservative suits or blazers and want them to appear more fashion-forward, wear them in unusual color mixes. If you want them to appear a touch less *all buttoned up,* "pull them apart". What you are creating is a "mixed suit" look— you use the jacket of one suit with the skirt or trousers of another, "marrying" them in interesting color combinations. To make these particular marriages work, you'll have to learn the *Secret Formula.* See *Smart Tip* #61.

42
Wearing the "In" Colors

How can you wear the touted "in" colors of the season and still look "okay"?

If you love to wear the "fashion" or "in" colors although they may not be enhancing to you, try to use your best *version* and clarity of these colors. You may be able to combine the latest "hues" with one of your best colors—keeping a great color next to your face can fool the eye, ensuring a more flattering look.

What about Khaki?

The color "khaki" has several incarnations—it has become a generic term for many shades of beige, tan, camel, light brown, and even some of these with green mixed in. So, when it comes to purchasing khaki trousers, for example, buy them in the *shade* that works best with your skin tone—believe me, it will never be one of those with a greenish cast. Don't forget to combine these "off-tones" with a color that is smashing on you!

43
Essential Accents

Colors that almost always need an accent near your face...

There are some colors that just work best when they are accented, near the face, with a touch of another color (sometimes the accent can be one of your best neutrals, as well). Not all of you will need this accent but here's the list to be suspicious of:

- beige, tan, and taupe,
- camel and khaki,
- brown,
- bronze,
- gray,
- rust,
- navy,
- pastels, and
- black.

Some colors to avoid in general

- taupe,
- putty,
- oatmeal,
- muddy or brownish grays,
- khaki,
- olive,
- very yellowish greens,
- oranges the color of pumpkins,
- mustard, and
- very orangy rusts.

If you do wear any of these colors, it's best to combine them in such a way that you end up with a color perfect accent near your face.

44

Make Sure You Look *Dazzling* in the Moonlight and the Candlelight!

Some of the colors listed above may work on you in the daytime without an accent but may require one at night. Night lighting can drain color out of your face—that's why adding a bit more makeup at night is often necessary. Think a.m. makeup and p.m. makeup!

Whenever you are buying something that you are planning to wear in the evening, find a dimly lit mirror (not hard in most stores) to check the color. If it fades-out or blacks-out (looks like a paler or darker color) you will probably look faded, too. No matter how beautiful the ensemble, it's not worth buying because *you* won't look beautiful in it exactly when you want to!

45

Consulting an "Expert"

A few words about "Color Consultants" and Image Consultants:

If you are not certain what colors and color combinations flatter you most, call Color 1 Associates at (202) 293-9175 for the number of the International Image and Style Consultant closest to you. Why am I recommending them? Because they have had the best training available anywhere in the world—they are my associates and they've all been trained by me, or by one of my really fabulous directors of training! Associates can also help you build the perfect *Smart* wardrobe for your current life or for the life of the woman you want to become. If there is not yet an associate near you, check the Resource Center for information on our Color 2000 charts.

Did you know that some "consultants" who **DO** color charts have had only 2 or 3 hours of color training and little or no wardrobe training? Most of their approximate 2-day training is on how to sell you makeup!

The Color 1 Associates that I recommend have studied approximately 4 weeks before their actual technical color training which lasts **6 full days** and is followed by a 3-Day Advanced Women's Wardrobe Training and an additional 2-Day Men's Wardrobe Training. An apprenticeship program follows their training.

The associates have paid up to $5,685 *plus* airfare, hotel and food expenses for their training versus the $250 or less that other companies charge for their 2-day "color" (makeup sales) training. We have recently made our training more affordable by separating actual training fees from supplies that we used to include. If you are interested in becoming a Color 1 Associate, check the Resource Center for the Director of Training closest to you.

46

Interpreting Patterns

If a pattern size is too small for you, it can make you look totally insignificant—the opposite of a **powerful**, successful image. If a pattern size is too large for you, it can completely **OVERPOWER** you, making you look washed-out by comparison. Don't be afraid of prints, plaids, and patterns, just learn which ones will flatter you!

Before we go into pattern size, here's another *very* important detail. All patterns should have at least two of your best colors prominent in them, AND the background color should also be flattering to you.

I'll bet you think that pattern size has to do with your height and size. Enhancing pattern size has to do with your body *coloring*. Yes, I know this is contrary to what you may believe, but it's true! Except for "placement", it has nothing to do with how tall you are or aren't, or with your size or shape.

Everyone can wear medium sized patterns but not everyone looks great in small patterns or large patterns. There are always a couple of "it depends upon".

If your coloring is more delicate looking, Gentle and Light-Bright Color Types, you'll look terrific in small and medium sized patterns, and (here's one of the "it depends upon") very lightweight, airy, delicate looking larger patterns that have a light background. If you are a Light-Bright Color Type, you will want to avoid small patterns that are *blended* looking (where all of the colors seem to run together).

Those of you who are Muted Color Types look great in medium sized patterns, small patterns that have some strength, and (another "it depends upon") very *blended* looking large patterns.

If you are a Contrast Color Type, medium and large patterns look wonderful on you. Small patterns that have extremely high contrast, like black with white and navy with white, can be effective if you accent them with a bright color, or with the dark color.

If you are a full-figured Contrast Color Type who is concerned about wearing large patterns, just be aware of *where* you place them on your body. If you are a petite Contrast Color Type and are worried that large patterns will overwhelm you, don't be! The proof will be in the compliments you get when you finally decide to wear a *color perfect* large pattern.

47

Dressing *Smart* in Dresses

Why is it that we see so few stylish dresses in the work place? One of the reasons is that there are so few good styles to choose from. Another is that many women seem to select dresses with a *different* part of their brain—the part that still wants to be a little girl, at a party, or living in another decade.

It's been said that a dress has to be very tailored looking to match the "authority" of a suit but it really only has to make *you* look great, stylish, elegant, and appropriate (remember your *Smart Tip*, **equal to or better than the best look you have right now**).

A dress that makes a statement equal to that of your best suit doesn't have to have a jacket but it does have to have all of the same wonderful qualities of that suit:

- The dress has presence and style;
- It is a style that is perfect for your workplace;
- It fits you well;
- Its fabric and construction are of good quality (it doesn't bag or sag after a few wearings);
- It's a great color on you;
- You've accessorized it perfectly; and
- You love it and are willing to wear it very often.

Dresses that come with matching or coordinating jackets are super, as are dresses that are styled so that you can wear one of your existing jackets over them. If you like a great deal of variety, look for a simple (*do not read: boring*) dress with beautiful lines that you can accessorize with different belts, scarves and necklaces. What does a dress like this look like?

- It's a solid color.
- It has a waistline (or shows a curve) at your natural waistline.
- Darts or curved seams make the top fairly fitted, like a well-tailored blouse.
- The neckline is one that will work with most of your jacket necklines and a variety of necklaces—a scoop, jewel, or "V" neck would be good.

- It could have tailored long-sleeves ("puffy" or fuller-cut sleeves are difficult under jackets), short-sleeves, or be sleeveless depending on the time of the year and your work/lifestyle.

- The skirt of the dress should be darted so that it fits well through the hips (like a well-tailored skirt), is pegged, and is in one of your favorite lengths.

- This "dress" could come in two pieces—it could actually be a *base* (a matching top and bottom) that you create out of a skirt and top. It could be that you already have the perfect "dress" already hanging in your closet.

In hot summer months when you may be tempted to wear a sleeveless dress to work, take a look around you. If you work in a conservative field where there is still a written or understood code against bare arms, play the "game" until you are in charge.

When you wear sleeveless dresses for work or play, make sure the armhole is cut high enough so that you cannot get even a glimpse of your bra or, heaven forbid, your bosom.

A dress, forgotten by many women, that is *phenomenally* easy to wear and stylish, too, is the two-piece dress with a straight skirt. Think of it as a skirt with a matching "tunic" top. It covers tummies, hips, unwanted bulges, and visible panty lines. If you make sure that the skirt is pegged, that your top isn't too long, and the shoulderline is a touch wider than your hipline (to give you that flattering "V" shape), you'll have a great look! The top doesn't have to be as long as a tunic, but if it is it should not be any longer than just barely covering your derriere.

Accessories can be kept to a minimum (or none, if you prefer) or you can go all out. Generally, it's not a good idea to belt a tunic. You can find these "dresses" in a huge variety of fabrics from silk to knits—catalogues are often a good source. Get the same ease and style with a tunic and matching narrow leg trousers.

48

Jacket Dressing

Jackets can create great style for an otherwise "ho-hum" ensemble. You rarely see a stylish Parisian or New York woman without one, even/especially when she is wearing jeans or other casual pants.

Personally, I collect jackets in various colors and styles and I definitely have more than I need. Do I wear them? Almost every day, both casual and dressy—they are one of my "signature statements". I definitely recommend that you *steal* your jackets off your "good" suits and wear them with your casual looks! Truthfully, I wouldn't have nearly so many if I didn't wait for them to be marked down to at least 50% to 75% off the **outlet** price!

There are lots of *Smart Tips* on jackets throughout this book—here are some more:

♦ Avoid wearing a "standard" classic blazer with sarong style skirt—a curvy shorter jacket would look great.

♦ A jacket/blazer of any style **rarely** looks wonderful over a dress with a drop-waist or a dress with a high waist that has the skirt fabric gathered onto the bodice. It is possible to wear some jacket styles over a classic "sheath" that has an empire waist (picture Audrey Hepburn).

♦ You can wear any style jacket whatever your size or height—all you have to do is pair a specific style with the right shape/style bottom.

♦ Wear narrower trousers and pegged skirts with all jacket styles.

- Longer jackets and classic blazers usually look more "contemporary" with narrow trousers and pegged skirts.
- Short, or very short, flared, flip or pleated skirts can work well with a large variety of jacket styles.
- Shorter jackets of all styles can be worn with almost all styles of trousers and skirts, including the pegged skirts and narrower cut trousers that work so well with longer jackets. Guess, then, which you should have more of in your wardrobe?

Classic blazers, both single and double-breasted, generally tend to be long enough to cover your derriere, and when they are paired with classic straight legged trousers (especially those that are a touch wide), they can shorten your leg line. Combining these two styles in contrasting colors can also make you look "broad" at the place the jacket ends.

Your full length mirror will tell you if this is happening; turn to the side to check—when your jacket and pants match, it's less noticeable than when they are two different colors. Be aware that it can also happen with tapered leg trousers because, although they taper to a narrower width toward your ankle, they can start overly wide at your upper leg. Put on heels and check the proportion again. It should be better—unless the heels have just made your pants too short in which case you've created another concern!

Consider changing the look of a jacket you haven't been wearing:

- Switch matching buttons to gold, silver or copper.
- Change metallic or odd colored buttons to matching buttons.
- Change buttons to match a "bottom" that hasn't been getting much use and you'll in-

stantly have a new suit—the buttons "tie" the two colors together.

- Add some curves to a boxy shaped jacket (a tailor can take in or add darts in the front and/or back).

- Put crystal or rhinestone buttons on a plain jacket to turn it into one that you can wear for cocktails and the theater.

49

Top Tops!

There is a true benefit to buying more tops than bottoms. A different top (i.e., blouse, sweater, shell, tank, camisole, etc.) can change the entire look/style, appropriateness or "flavor" of an ensemble allowing you to have "zillions" of outfits with a minimal investment in skirts and trousers. Be sure to include some tops you *feel* sexy in and one top with a "zillion" buttons in the front—a friend reports that in certain situations prolonged anticipation is a delightful aphrodisiac.

Some details to be aware of:

- Blouses without pockets are more "basic" because they can be worn under more styles/cuts of jackets. Sometimes the edge of a pocket will show when you have your jacket on, requiring either a change of your top or jacket.

- We all need to be aware of pockets that are too low, but this is a special concern for petites. Low pockets can make you look like your bosom is low or, *yikes*, droopy.

- Styles that work best with all of your jackets are simple long sleeved, short-sleeved and sleeveless shells, tanks, crew necks, scoop/

rounded/V/U-necks, and fine quality T-shirts.

- Turtlenecks and mock turtlenecks will work with many jacket styles as well.

- Be aware that the texture of ribbed knits is much more limiting than knits that have a "smooth" or flat finish.

- Tops in prints can add wonderful variety but they are useless unless they contain the colors of your "bottoms".

- Take note of where short-sleeved tops hit on your arm. If they end too low, they may cause your bosom to look low/droopy. If they end exactly at the fullest part of your bosom, they can make you look more ample—fine for some.

- Silk, rayon, fine cotton, merino wool, lightweight cashmere, micro fibers, and finely textured knits are great fabrics for tops.

- Avoid anything scratchy!

- There's more information on tops in your *Smart Capsule* class.

50
Keeping Effort to a Minimum

If your blouses seem to always need ironing, spend most of their time at the cleaners, or do not work well with the necklines of most of your jackets, you could just **stop buying them**! Purchase instead the most versatile tops listed above.

It's always a good idea to follow the laundering instructions on the labels of all of your clothing, and I think you should! But, *I'm just going to whisper in your ear* that I, personally, wash all of my tops made out of the fabrics listed above in cold water on the gentle cycle in my machine.

Yes, I wash all my silks and cashmere, but of all of the fabrics listed above, rayon is the one that I hesitate to wash because it might shrink. I also hesitate to launder tops that are lined, because the lining can shrink. If you take your tops out of the washer right away, most (except blouses) won't need any ironing or just a touch-up to make the silk and cotton feel silky and soft instead of "crunchy".

If you forget to take them out soon enough, you can put them in the dryer for a couple of minutes on delicate. Use padded hangers to avoid hanger marks at the shoulder and "block" (stretch) knits that need it— my arms are long so I pull on the sleeves to keep the length I need. There are some wonderful "pads" available that you can place on a regular hanger that gives the same shape as your shoulders (they are adjustable so they work for different shoulder widths). I use them in my closet for my knit dresses and knit tops as well as in the laundry room. Check the Resource Center for how to order them.

51

Have You Ever Considered If Your Arms Match Your Body?

Many women avoid sleeveless tops—they feel that their upper arms are too *generous* to show. One of my full-figured clients was going on her first cruise and I was pre-shopping for her (shopping without her) because she had so little time to spare before her departure. When I asked her how she felt about sleeveless tops, she said that she didn't wear them because...

I suggested that she try on a sleeveless shell (that she always covers with a jacket) and look in the mirror and ask herself if her arms "go with" her body. Her answer? "Yes!" Of course, she now loves wearing sleeveless dresses and tops in the summer—but not to work because she works in a fairly conservative field.

Tops that "fit" often (but not always) work better with trousers that have a big or loose cut, like cargo pants and some of those with drawstrings, than they do with fuller cut tops. "Fit" doesn't have to mean tight, just cut fairly close to the body. Big, loose tops paired with "baggy" bottoms can end up making you look sloppy instead of chic. *Mirror check!*

52

Getting Your Necklines Coordinated...

Wearing a notched collar blouse with a shawl collar jacket does both an injustice. One easy rule is to have the neckline of your blouse or top repeat the same line as your jacket. Here are some *Smart Tips*:

- ◆ Jewel, scoop, "U", and just slightly rounded necklines work well with most all jacket styles, which makes them very versatile.
- ◆ A "V" neckline works well with notched collar lapels and collarless jackets that also have a "V" shape.
- ◆ A blouse with a notched collar goes well with most notched collar jackets and works even better if the "notches" fall into line or if the notch of one fills in the space between the notches of the other.
- ◆ Some notched collars come to a "point" and others are rounded-off. *Please* don't mix them.
- ◆ It usually looks best if the notched collar on a blouse is a little narrower than the notched collar on your jacket.
- ◆ Blouses with a shawl collar are great with a shawl collar suit as are jewel, scoop, and U-shaped necklines.

53

Sweater Girl

What about wearing sweaters to work?

The easy answer is sure you can, but not *too* tight. Nothing is that easy because you always have to deal with the "it depends on…" stuff.

First, let's talk about long sweaters—the kind that many of us love to wear for casual attire with leggings. For the past few years, fashion editors have told us that leggings are out. Stores kept selling them and women kept wearing them because they are *sooooooo* comfortable. Paired with a long sweater, they *hide* tummies that aren't flat and derrieres and upper legs that aren't as firm as one might wish.

Seriously, what seems to have happened is that women started taking "license" with leggings. They wore them (anywhere and everywhere, including to work) with baggy stretched-out sweaters or with shorter sweaters as if they were a regular pair of pants instead of a garment that more closely resembles "very thick footless pantyhose". What *everyone* saw, especially from the back, was a view that was rarely flattering. No wonder the "fashion police" tried to outlaw them!

Currently, they are "back", and when you wear them I want you to look stylish and appropriate. If you consider leggings and a **long** sweater a great, casual look for you, go for it as long as you can promise me that you look **GREAT!**

Please don't be tempted to wear them when the look isn't to your advantage. When in doubt, instead of leggings try a pair of really narrow leg pants made out of a micro fiber—very stylish and totally comfortable!

If you are a fan of long sweaters, make sure that those you are wearing are not *too* long for you—if they are, they'll shorten your leg line. To help offset this, wear shoes or boots with heels. Say no to sweaters that "cup" under your derriere.

As a matter of course, the best shape for a long sweater is one that hangs straight down without the type of ribbing that makes it smaller around at the bottom. With a long skirt, the best proportion for most women will be with a sweater **no longer** than just barely covering her derriere. Again, heels can help the balance. Also try this length with short pegged skirts and, "once in a fashion while", with fuller skirts.

With pants, especially, a sweater that falls below your derriere makes a more casual statement. With skirts, it depends on the fabrics and the overall look whether you will look fashionable, trendy, casual, or sloppy.

54

More "It Depends Upon"

A cardigan is a terrific option to a jacket *if* it looks substantial and elegant—substantial meaning "weighty" and more structured versus a thinner merino wool cardigan that might be part of a twin-set, for example. Judge it by your *Smart Tip*, if it looks **equally as smashing as your best jacket**, wear it to work!

Although they do not take the place of a jacket, twin-sets are great for many places of business and are "dressier" than just a sweater.

"Outdoorsy" looking sweaters and sweaters with lots of glitz are usually best kept for your free time unless you work in an environment where you know that they are expected and accepted attire. I would expect to see you wearing a ski sweater if you work in an outdoor sports shop that sells ski wear or backpacking and camping equipment. And, I wouldn't be at all surprised to see you in a sweater with glitz if you work in a boutique that sells like objects!

This doesn't mean that those of you who work in more conservative fields cannot wear sweaters that are "embellished". There are some great sweaters that are embroidered, have a few pearls or simple, subtle studs that you may be able to wear to your place of business. If you want to make something embellished look more conservative, keep everything else you are wearing very simple and understated.

Obviously, sweaters under jackets are great for even the most conservative workplace, but if you still aren't certain about wearing just a sweater without a jacket, observe what the top women in your company are wearing and follow their lead until you get to be the leader. **Exception: follow no frumpy or dowdy leaders.**

Some cowl neck sweaters, dolman sleeves, and drop-shoulder sleeves can make your shoulderline look narrower than it is, so consider adding small shoulder pads. Large cowl neck styles can also make a small head look even smaller in proportion to body size and it can make a slender neck look "scrawny".

Boleros and shrugs come and go in fashion. And, yes, shrugs do tend to accentuate your bosom.

Tying sweaters around your hips isn't a stylish look. It is a look that makes your hips look larger, and therefore, your shoulders look smaller. The only time this look "works" is *during* athletics when you start out cold and you end up warm, or vice versa.

55
The Age-Old Debate About Hemlines

Look at your legs and decide how much of them you want to show-off. Look at the business you are in and decide if short skirts and really short skirts fit with your career goals. Take a third look, and decide if you look stylish and elegant in them.

How much longer is a short skirt than a very short skirt? I can't tell you in inches, because 2" on short legs gives a much shorter appearance than on longer legs. But here's a fun guideline:

- ◆ Measure the distance between the top of your kneecap and your crotch—mine is 12".

- ◆ The place on your leg that is ½ of that distance is approximately where a **very** short skirt might end—for me that is 6" above my kneecap.

- ◆ ¼ of your original measurement will give you the approximate place where your short skirt might end—for me it is 3" above my kneecap.

At this point, you may find it helpful to skip to the *Smart Tips* on shoes and boots, #66, and stockings, #75, and then come back here to go over these general guidelines—they'll help you in deciding which stockings, and which weight and style of shoe, will work best with a specific skirt length.

A "short story"…

Just a few years ago I was prompted to write my first letter to an editor of one of our major fashion magazines. Having just returned from the "shows", she wrote in the lead-in to the magazine's main fashion section that the newest skirt length, one that was a few inches below the knee, was fabulous and that *any other skirt length looked passé.*

Now, I know that a long time ago WE stopped letting fashion editors and designers dictate what our skirt lengths should be in order for us to look fashionable. This editor's comment sounded not only dictatorial to me, but it made me furious. Why? Because she'd just told every American woman that unless she goes out and spends her hard earned money on this new length (and tosses out all of her old lengths), she will look out of style—out of date! I was hoping that nobody took the time to read this editorial and it seems that most of you either missed it or that you chose to ignore her—**Thank you!**

My letter to her explained that instead of trying to, once again, dictate our skirt lengths, it would have been so much nicer if she had let us know that we now have an *additional* choice, and had explained *how* to best wear the new length (with very sheer stockings and heels).

56

Getting *Smarter*

- Skirts that hover around your knee, from just above the kneecap to just below, need a medium to light-weight shoe and fairly sheer stockings.

- Lengths that fall from just below the kneecap to 2" or 3" below will look much more stylish with at least a mid-height heel and sheer stockings (either nude/skin tone or a sheer tint of neutral that matches your shoe or skirt—no opaques with this length, *please*).

- Generally, the shorter the skirt, the heavier the shoe *could* be (a medium weight is always appropriate)—but a light-weight skirt fabric (in any length) calls for a medium to lighter weight shoe.

- Generally, the longer the skirt, the lighter weight the shoe. Note that I did not say to wear a light-weight shoe necessarily, just that as the hemline drops, the weight of the shoe "usually" drops as well (again, the weight of the skirt fabric will affect the appropriate shoe weight).

- A pump with a slender heel and low vamp and side is always appropriate with skirts from just above the knee to the floor. Depending on the look you want to create and where you are going, this shoe will also work with a short skirt. And, also "depending on", a low cut flat will work.

♦ Delicate and light-weight fabrics always need light to medium weight shoes.

♦ Heavier weight fabrics do not necessarily need more weight in a shoe—it depends on the length of your skirt. When in doubt, a medium weight shoe will always be appropriate with heavier fabrics.

♦ Avoid spike heels with very short skirts unless this is a stylish look for your lifestyle.

♦ Avoid chunky or clunky-looking shoes unless you are wearing a short or very short skirt and creating a specific trendy look that calls for them.

Very long skirts are fabulous, but what is "stylishly" long and what is *too* long for daytime? An inch or two above the ankle bone is usually long enough for the daytime. I love really long skirts (and short skirts, too) but when a skirt comes all the way down almost to the floor it can make you look like you're engulfed in fabric or living in another time. Use your mirror to help you decide—does your attire look out of place for your place of business? Do you look elegant or enveloped?

If your skirt appears just a little too long, try wearing it with a heel (shoe or boot) to raise the hem, creating more inches between the bottom of the skirt and the floor. Now take another look. If it still looks too long, it should be shortened—maybe only 1"!

There's sort of a "no man's land" for skirt lengths—aptly named because most men don't pay attention to women who wear their skirts this length. The reason this length often looks dowdy is because women don't know "how" to make it look more chic. The length in question? From 2" or 3" below the kneecap to 2" or 3" above the anklebone—it depends on your height and your leg length. Remember, 2" looks a lot *more* on a woman who is 5' 2" than it does on one who is 5' 9".

The very best way to look stylish in these "difficult" lengths is to wear very sheer stockings and high heels. In the fall and winter, you can also wear boots (best with opaque stockings) making certain, unless you're creating a trendy, arty or eccentric look, that the hem covers the top of the boot when you walk. Don't forget that skirts can also be shortened to a more flattering length.

Women of every height can look great in both long and short skirts—it's all a matter of getting the skirt long enough or short enough; getting the shape right (pegged, for example); knowing what style top and/or jacket to combine the length with; and determining what stockings and shoe or boot style finishes the look perfectly for *you*.

57

Trouser Style

When trousers look good, they look very, very good, and when they look bad, they're horrid!

You've already read many *Smart Tips* about how to create a longer leg, to avoid spreading pockets and spreading pleats, etc. The *Smart Tips* in "shoes and boots", #66, will help you with trouser styles and lengths and their best weight of footwear. Here are some more guidelines:

- The wider the trousers, the longer they should be—1" off the floor in the back (with your shoes/boots on) is an elegant length.

- More classic widths and narrower straight legged trousers should end no *higher* than the place where the heel of the shoe meets the main body of the shoe.

- Narrower cut trousers that taper toward the ankle are worn a little shorter (because they are smaller around the ankle, they won't be able to come down over the shoe any fur-

ther)—they should still definitely cover the
ankle bone; some have a slit on the side that
helps makes this possible.

- A slight break in the front of your trousers is
  always nice.

- It's very difficult to look *smart* and stylish in
  cropped pants even when they are "in" because they are so unflattering to the leg and
  ankle.

- Bell bottoms are to be worn very long, but
  not worn at all if you wore them when you
  were "younger".

- If you've "done" bell bottoms, bootleg cut
  are a better bet—wear them long.

- Capris (short and tapered, ending from just
  below the knee to mid-calf) come and go in
  fashion, and like bell bottoms, you may want
  to avoid them "the second time around".

- Cuffs are classic. Please make sure your cuffed
  pants are long.

- Trousers that are designed to fit with a bit of
  ease shouldn't be tight across your derriere
  or around your upper legs.

- Both pleated and flat front trousers are classic and can be worn by **all** women.

- Trousers that are cut narrower in the leg (versus wide) are the most flattering to **all** women
  and they work well with all jacket styles

- Leggings—it's how you wear them—see
  Smart Tip #53.

58

Building a *Smart* Wardrobe

How much of your wardrobe do you *really* use?
Two of the reasons why most women only wear
about 25% of their wardrobe in any given season is

that their closets are full of separates that don't go together and/or they don't know how to combine the pieces to create great looking outfits.

To solve the first, get in the habit of buying entire ensembles—that doesn't mean that you must buy all of the pieces that were made to go together, although that's (usually) a nice easy way to look coordinated, but not as original as some of you may like. No matter what, *please, please*, always buy the matching top to any skirt or trousers you are purchasing, so that when worn together they make a *base*. Or, look for a matching top made by any other manufacturer right away—I'm sure that you've noticed that certain colors are prevalent in any given season and it will be much easier to find the exact shade you need if you're looking for it in the same season. For example:

If you buy a yellow skirt, buy a *basic* matching yellow top; buy a purple top to match the purple trousers you bought two years ago but haven't yet worn; and while you are at it, see if your cream colored sleeveless shell matches the skirt of your cream-colored suit.

The easiest way to start to build a *Smart Wardrobe* is to keep your look uncomplicated and understated (do not read: boring)—you can branch out and go "wild" (or just a little wilder) once you get your wardrobe working for you. Remember, quality, not quantity. Well tailored. Wonderful colors, in your best clarity, and super color combinations for you.

59

Creating a *Smart* "Base"!

There's that word again—by now you know that it means a matching top and bottom, and you've probably gotten the idea that I feel that you should have as many as you can. You're right!

A *base* is an "all one color look" made by combining a *basic* skirt or trousers with a matching *basic* blouse, tank, camisole, shell, simple sweater, or any other plain (again, do not read: boring) top. How close do the colors have to match? They can be a hint lighter or darker but they need to be close enough so that, at a glance, they look like they are the same color. Having several *smart bases* allows you to have a *Smart Wardrobe*—it's **by far** the easiest way in the world to look well-coordinated and elegant.

60

Transforming Your *Smart* Base!

You can change the look of your *smart* base simply by what you choose to wear on top of it:

- Different colors and styles of jackets,
- Vests,
- Tunics,
- Sweaters,
- Cardigans,
- Another shirt,
- Belts,
- Scarves, and
- Different accessories.

Please keep in mind your best color combinations.

The top and bottom that create your *base* should be both *basic,* and generally, classic. Basic because they can be easily combined with so many other garments, and classic because you can wear them for many years. Just a change of a jacket style or accessories can instantly update classic *bases*, keeping them *stylish*.

Collect *bases* for work, play, and romantic evenings, in all the different fabrics and colors you love. I love my denim *base* equally as well as I love my linen, wool, and silk *bases*. Try a blue jeans *base* and a cream denim *base*—wear them with shoes/boots and belt in your hair color (yes, your hair color—much more about this concept in "shoes and boots", Tip #66) and count the compliments! You will always look more "dressed-up" in a *base*, even in denim, than you do in unmatched separates.

61
Mixing it Up

Create entirely different outfits by wearing the bottom of one base with the top of another—to "balance" these combinations requires bringing the bottom color "up", your *Secret Formula* for having a great *pulled-together* look. Use a variety of jacket, top, trouser, and skirt styles—each will increase the individuality of your look and you'll have an excellent start on building a great *Smart Capsule Wardrobe*.

Learning how to combine separates to create great looking outfits is fun, and not really that difficult—like learning a new "trick" on your computer that will make your life easier forever (for me, it was learning how to use "search").

Bringing the bottom color "up"

An astonishingly simple way to have a pulled-together look is to bring the bottom color of your outfit "up". This easy feat allows you to marry separates that you would never have believed could be combined into unique and great looking outfits.

One of the easiest ways to accomplish this is to own neck accessories in the colors of your "bottoms"—your skirts and trousers. Plan a special shopping expedition where you only look for necklaces and solid colored scarves that match all of your favorite bottoms.

For example, if you own pink linen trousers and you've only been wearing them with a cream top, find matching pink beads/pearls or a matching pink scarf. Now you can wear your trousers with many different colored tops—just add your pink neck accessory and watch the beautiful *balance/coordination* take place.

While you are shopping, you can also keep an eye out for scarves and necklaces that have a **fairly large** amount of these colors—just a touch usually isn't enough to create the needed visual *balance*. Do a "mirror test" to make sure that your neck accessory *obviously pulls* the bottom color "up" from a DISTANCE, not just up close.

The minute you find any neck accessory to match one of your bottoms, start putting this principle to work right away. Try on your skirt or trousers with a *basic* top in a different color—one that has a neckline that is compatible with your new necklace or scarf (don't forget to keep in mind your best color combinations). Before you add the neck accessory, look in the mirror. At this point, depending on the colors you are combining, you may **not** have a very coordinated looking ensemble.

Now, add your accessory (you are "bringing the bottom color up") and take another look—"instant balance", beautifully coordinated looking! Now, if you like, be daring and add a jacket in a third color (again, make sure your necklines work well together). Take yet another look—even in this three-color combination, you will still look very pulled-together!

Whenever you buy a new "bottom", immediately look for a matching neck accessory because *bringing the bottom color "up"* is the **KEY** to mixing, matching and marrying separates. Here are some other ways to bring the bottom color up:

- A belt and shoe in the same color;
- A scarf or necklace the same color as your belt; and
- A top the same color as the skirt or trousers— *a smart base.*

What about using a jacket, vest or cardigan to bring the bottom color up? Absolutely, but it only counts *if* you are certain that you'll leave it on. Earrings are usually not "enough" to create the balance you need, and if your hair covers them, they don't help at all. Avoid dotting color here and there, jumping from your shoes all the way to your neck or ear. For instance, red shoes and red necklace or earrings, with nothing red between, can look too spotty and/or too matchy-pooh!

Sometime your hair color can act as a neck accessory would. If your hair is very dark brown or black and you are wearing black trousers with a top in one of your colors, your hair color can appear to bring the bottom color up. If your hair color is blond and you are wearing a camel skirt with cream (or one of your light colors) your hair color can create the balance you need to look "pulled-together".

If you don't want to go the "bottom color up" avenue (perhaps you're not a scarf or necklace person), or you haven't yet found your matching accessories, what else can you do to get more of your separates to work together? Wearing colors that have like "values" (two light colors together, for example) can create a well coordinated, balanced appearance without really needing to bring the bottom color up. Keeping your best color combinations in mind, here are some examples—combine:

- A light color with another light color like pastel yellow with pastel blue or cream with light gray (if your coloring is strong, you may need to add a medium or dark accent);
- A medium color with another medium color like medium turquoise with a camel;
- Or a dark color with another dark color like navy with dark raspberry (if your coloring is delicate looking you will need to "lighten-up" these darker color combinations—or just avoid them).

It's also possible to get fairly good balance by wearing white, off-white, or cream with light colors and by wearing black, charcoal gray, or navy with medium toned colors—again, *please* keep your best color combinations in mind.

Although like values of colors balance each other, it is *always* appropriate (and fantastic looking) to bring the bottom color "up". For those of you who love them, just think of how much fun it's going to be to finally wear neck accessories that really work! For those of you who don't want to be bothered with any of this, the solution is easy—always wear a *base*.

62

Creating a *Smart Capsule* Wardrobe

Some women wish they had a "uniform" (like men do) because they'd know exactly what to put on in the morning without the last minute STRESS of trying to figure out what goes with what. If you want to simplify your life and still look great every day, *continue...*

How would you like to look not only professional but fabulous every working day for an entire month and never wear the same outfit twice? Sound expensive? It's not! Here's the "formula"—2 + 2 + 5 = 20:

- ◆ 2 basic suits (or 2 jackets and 2 skirts/trousers),
- ◆ 2 neck accessories (solid colored scarves or necklaces) that match your skirts/trousers, and
- ◆ 5 basic tops.

The suits

Use two *basic* suits, or two jackets and two skirts/trousers ("mixed suit" looks), whose jackets and skirts/trousers can be interchanged so that the jacket of one can be worn with the skirt/trousers of the other and vice versa. Choose solid colors, your best colors of course, and **keep in mind your most flattering color combinations.**

If your workplace is *highly* conservative, you may not be as adventuresome as you could be in selecting the colors for your capsule. But, starting out with one jacket in a neutral (off-white, cream, beige, camel, brown, rust, navy, gray, and black) and one in a color, will give you some great variety—the "bottoms", as mentioned above, can match the jackets or not.

The neck accessories

Used to "bring the bottom color up", the color of the neck accessory **IS CRITICAL** and the main reason the capsule works! You will need a necklace or solid color scarf to match each of your skirts/trousers.

For example, navy colored or lapis beads to match a navy skirt; pearls or a cream-colored scarf to match a cream-colored skirt; a camel scarf to match camel trousers; a red necklace or scarf to match a red skirt, and so on.

The five *basic* tops

Use uncomplicated blouses, shells, tanks, crew-necks, or pullovers. All five tops must compliment your suits or mixed suit looks from a color, texture and a compatible neckline standpoint. The more uncomplicated the top (do not read: boring), the better. For example, a pullover in a smooth or flat-weave knit is much more versatile than one that is ribbed and a blouse without pockets works with more jacket styles.

For more variety in your tops you may use a combination of solid colors and prints. However, any print must contain **both** of the jacket colors and **both** of the colors of your skirts/trousers.

For instance, if you have built your capsule around two solid color suits, one in cream and one in red, your print top must have both the *exact* shades of cream and red. If your capsule is built around a black suit, red jacket, and camel trousers, your print tops must contain black, red, **and** camel.

The styling

You'll want to be certain that your jackets and skirts/trousers work well with each other from a style perspective. For example, if one of your jackets is long, your skirts will most likely need to be pegged and your trousers cut with a narrow leg. If both jackets are shorter, you can more easily combine them with a variety of skirt and trouser styles.

To make your life simple, the buttons on your capsule jackets should match the color of the jackets exactly, otherwise, they can interfere with your neck accessory. What if one of your jackets already has great looking gold or silver buttons on it? Can you work around them? Yes, but the metallic color of the buttons usually needs to be "tied-in" to your necklace. For example, if one of your jackets has gold buttons on it and you are wearing it with a contrasting skirt/trousers (often necessitating bringing the bottom color "up"), your necklace will also need to have some gold beads in it to look beautifully coordinated. If it doesn't, try twisting a gold necklace (usually a simple chain) around your capsule necklace.

Those of you who wear more trendy/fashion-forward, ethnic, arty, or eccentric looks can create a capsule with more avant-garde pieces of clothing and accessories. And, those of you who work in casual workplaces can use more casual pieces like jeans, khakis, and cotton T's to create a casual capsule.

The fabrics

All of your capsule "pieces" must work well together from a fabric standpoint. You may want to review the information on fabrics in *Smart Tip #65*.

How does the capsule work?

Essentially what you are going to be doing is wearing all five tops with each of your skirts or trousers, switching jackets and always making sure that you reach for the neck accessory in the color of your "bottom".

Smart Capsule for Delicate Coloring

If your best clarity is clear and bright, yet delicate looking, every color in the capsule would be in this clarity. On the other hand, if your best clarity is more subdued and toned-down, every color in the capsule would be in that clarity.

You can use any of your best *shades* of colors for your capsule as long as you are creating color combinations that are wonderful on you. The colors in this capsule were simply chosen at random, but the color combinations are **specifically** flattering to delicate coloring!

As you read through the following combinations, if you look best in clear colors, imagine the suit in a clear pink. If toned-down colors are great on you, imagine the suit in a more subdued, gentle looking pink. The same goes for all of the colors of your tops, of course.

The pieces

Suit with a skirt:	Pink
Mixed suit look:	Camel jacket and light gray trousers

5 Tops:	Pink jewel neck blouse
	Light gray silk pullover
	Yellow scoop-neck shell
	Cream V-neck blouse with matching buttons
	Light blue-purple rayon T-shirt

Don't forget that the necklines of your tops must be compatible with both jacket styles and work well with both of your neck accessories.

2 Neck Accessories:	Pink scarf (solid color)
	Gray pearls

Shoes:	Camel
	Gray

1 — Pink suit with pink blouse and pink scarf (optional),

2 — Pink jacket with gray trousers, cream blouse, and gray pearls,

3 — Camel jacket with pink skirt, yellow shell, and pink scarf,

4 — Pink jacket with gray trousers, yellow shell, and gray pearls,

5 — Camel jacket with gray trousers, purple T-shirt, and gray pearls,

6 — Pink suit with purple T-shirt and pink scarf,

7 — Camel jacket with pink skirt, cream blouse, and pink scarf,

8 — Camel jacket with gray trousers, yellow shell, and gray pearls,

9 — Pink jacket with gray trousers, purple T-shirt, and gray pearls,

10 — Pink suit with yellow blouse and pink scarf,

11 — Camel jacket with gray trousers, cream blouse, and gray pearls,

12 — Camel jacket with pink skirt, purple T-shirt, and pink scarf,

13 — Pink jacket with gray trousers, gray pullover, and gray pearls (optional),

14 — Pink jacket with gray trousers, pink blouse, and gray pearls,

15 — Camel jacket with gray trousers, gray pullover, and gray pearls (optional),

16 — Camel jacket with gray trousers, pink blouse, and gray pearls,

17 — Pink suit with gray pullover and pink scarf,

18 — Pink suit with cream blouse and pink scarf,

19 — Camel jacket with pink skirt, pink blouse and pink scarf (optional), and

20 — Camel jacket with pink skirt, gray pullover, and pink scarf.

Smart Capsule for Strong Coloring

If your best clarity is clear, bright and bold, all of the colors in this capsule will be in this clarity. On the other hand, if your best clarity is slightly toned-down and subdued, all of the colors will be in that clarity.

You can use any of your best shades of colors as long as you are creating color combinations that look great on you. The colors in this capsule were simply chosen at random, but are **specific** examples of color combinations that will flatter strong coloring.

As you read through the following combinations, if you look great in clear colors, imagine a clear, bright red suit; and if you look super in more toned-down colors, imagine a more subdued, muted red suit. The same with all of your colors of tops, of course.

Because this "fictitious" capsule is for both women who can wear the high contrast of black and white together and those who cannot, I have used the softer contrast color combination of beige with black. If you are a woman who can wear high contrast, if you wish, you may substitute in white, off-white or cream for the beige.

The pieces

Suit with a skirt:	Red
Mixed suit look:	Beige jacket and black trousers (if you don't look good in black, substitute in navy)
5 Tops:	Red jewel neck blouse
	Black silk pullover
	Purple V-neck shell
	Yellow rayon T-shirt
	Beige scoop neck blouse

Please don't forget that the necklines of all five tops must be compatible with both jacket styles and with your neck accessories.

Neck accessories:	Red scarf
	Black beads
Shoes:	Black
	Red

1 — Red suit with red blouse and red scarf (optional),

2 — Beige jacket with black trousers, red blouse, and black beads,

3 — Red jacket with black trousers, black pullover, and black beads (optional),

4 — Beige jacket with red skirt, purple shell, and red scarf,

5 — Beige jacket with black trousers, yellow T-shirt, and black beads,

6 — Red suit with black blouse and red scarf,

7 — Red jacket with black trousers, beige blouse, and black beads,

8 — Beige jacket with red skirt, yellow T-shirt, and red scarf,

9 — Beige jacket with black trousers, black pullover, and black beads (optional),

10 — Red suit with beige blouse and red scarf,

11 — Beige jacket with black trousers, beige blouse, and black beads,

12 — Beige jacket with black trousers, purple shell, and black beads,

13 — Red suit with purple shell and red scarf,

14 — Red suit with yellow T-shirt and red scarf,

15 — Beige jacket with red skirt, beige blouse, and red scarf,

16 — Beige jacket with red skirt, black pullover, and red scarf,

17 — Beige jacket with red skirt, red blouse, and red scarf (optional),

18 — Red jacket with black trousers, red blouse, and black beads,

19 — Red jacket with black trousers, purple shell, and black beads, and

20 — Red jacket with black trousers, yellow T-shirt, and black beads.

Each capsule also makes 10 different looks without a jacket. How different do you look without the jacket? Try it and see; you'll be surprised at the difference and you might just have discovered some great looks for "dress-down days"!

63
Adding the "Spice" of Variety

To give variety to your capsule, add patterned scarves—they **must** contain the colors that you are combining that day. For example, if you are wearing gray trousers, a yellow top, and a pink jacket, your scarf will include gray, yellow, and pink. If you're wearing red, purple, and black, a scarf with those colors in it would be super!

More variety comes with the addition of a print blouse that has your main item capsule colors of pink, camel, and gray, or in the case of the strong capsule, red, black, and beige.

Note that in these capsules I've included tops that match each bottom—automatically giving you two *bases*, which makes it easy for you to extend your capsule by wearing them with most any other odd jacket. Note, also, that the neck accessory is optional when you are wearing a base because you have already "brought-up" the bottom color. If you are wearing jackets with matching bottoms, the neck accessory is also optional **IF** you keep your jacket *on.*

64
Feed Your Closet *Smartly—* Don't Stuff It

When many women shop they just "fatten" their closets with miscellaneous "stuff" that doesn't go with anything else. If you go and look in your closet (I'd like you to think of it as a shop called, "Your Favorite Boutique") right now, most of you will find that you already have the "pieces" to create at least one *Smart Capsule Wardrobe* and you didn't even know it! Therefore, your closet is the best place to "shop"—for FREE—to add super items to your capsule.

By carefully adding just 1 jacket, 1 bottom, 1 top, and 1 neck accessory that go with your *capsule*, you can make countless different looks! Remember that necklines, styles, colors, and fabrics must be compatible and your neck accessory needs to be the color of your new bottom. Your additions don't have to go with every single thing in the capsule—it would be terrific if they even coordinated with just a few of the other pieces!

More *smart* details

Turn one of your capsule suits into an evening look by adding a silk or lace camisole, or wear a dressy jacket over one of your *bases*. This works best if the fabrics are dressier, like a wool or rayon crepe, wool gabardine, silk, or even one of the micro fibers. A change of accessories, if necessary, and you're off! If you attend many evening functions, consider creating an evening capsule.

Add uniqueness through your accessories. Just because you have a red scarf to balance a red skirt doesn't mean that you won't want to keep your eyes open for a red necklace. Also, remember to collect patterned scarves in your capsule colors. On the days where you are wearing one of your bases, leave off the optional accessory and add a great belt!

65

Change the Fabric, Change the Style

Fabric is amazing! Just picture your favorite "businesslike" pantsuit in a totally different fabric, a brocade, for example, or velvet. It can change the look of a subtle classic into a rare and exotic treasure! Here are some things about fabrics that you might like to know:

Knits are super for business wear for **all** body types as long as they are not too tight. Those that are too clingy can show bulges above and below your bra, and at the waist and hips. Some of the new "body slimming" slips, panties and stockings can help *smooth-out* this concern, as can camisoles and slips that help knit fabrics glide over the body instead of clinging to it.

Fabrics that bag and sag ruin the look of an otherwise great outfit. Avoid purchasing inexpensive rayons and inexpensive knits unless you are willing to give them up after one season. Wearing a slip will help them hold their shape, as will not wearing them to death.

Sheer and "peek-a-boo" fabrics are not generally considered businesslike; well, maybe "monkey businesslike". How sheer is "too sheer"? You get to judge. Does it work if you wear a camisole under it? Only you know your place of business, its spoken and unspoken "codes", and your career goals. When in doubt, save "it" for playtime.

Cotton-polyester knits are too casual if you work in a law firm, but they are probably perfect for you if you work in the office of a veterinarian, or if you are a doctor of veterinarian medicine. When you try something on and you *feel* casual or sporty in it, do not wear it for business attire unless sporty/casual is the look you are striving for.

For the budget conscious, or those who like a sparse wardrobe, buy garments in fabrics that you can wear year-round in your climate. Consider:

- Silks, including raw silks;
- Tropical weight woolens;
- Good quality rayons;
- Micro fibers;
- Knits; and
- Blends of synthetic and natural fibers.

Silks can be worn day and night all year long in our warmer climates. In areas with four more distinct seasons, in cold weather months, silk ensembles generally get relegated to evening wear. In other words, the silk pantsuit you wore to work all summer could be used for a cocktail party in the winter—with a change of accessories, perhaps.

Similar weights of fabrics easily balance each other, like combining two light-weight fabrics. It's also possible to combine most light-weight fabrics with medium weight fabrics and most medium weight fabrics with heavier weight fabrics.

If you try to combine a heavier wool flannel jacket with a wool crepe skirt/trousers, you may throw your balance off—it can depend on how "substantial" the crepe looks, the lining and the color combination. When balance is thrown off in this way, sometimes the less-substantial fabric can end up looking inexpensive—even if it isn't. This outfit has a better chance of working if the heavier fabric is on the bottom and the lighter on the top.

It's best for delicate color types to avoid really rough, coarse, and very heavy looking textures.

66

Are We in the Decade of the "Ugly" Shoe?

Although there are really beautiful shoes available, it seems that many women are buying the ugly ones. What makes a shoe ugly? Well, some are just that way, but others only *look* ugly because they are being worn with clothing styles that call for a different shoe—usually a lighter weight shoe.

The biggest mistake, by far, is wearing a shoe, slide/mule, or sandal that is too heavy for the outfit. I know that you see these looks in magazines and catalogs but that doesn't mean it looks good. Yes, what I'm saying is that many of the designers and stylists **don't know** (hopefully it's not because they just don't care) that this look is unflattering, unbalanced, totally unsophisticated, and makes your feet look big.

67

EXPLODING the "Myth" that a Black Shoe is Always Appropriate

One of my favorite sites in Washington is the Thomas Jefferson Memorial. Inscribed on the walls are some of Jefferson's quotes, including (I'm paraphrasing) the observation that just because something has been done a certain way for a long time doesn't mean that it's right for today—and it doesn't mean that it was **ever** right!

Somewhere along the way, women were taught erroneously that they could wear black shoes with anything. That's not accurate now, it never was, and it never will be unless your hair is black or very dark brown.

Example: Four women—a caramel blond, a brunette, a redhead, and one with very, very dark brown or black hair—are all wearing a medium-toned blue dress and skin tone/nude stockings. Close your eyes and "picture" each wearing black shoes. Only the very dark brown or black-haired woman will look well coordinated—pulled-together, finished, polished!

Now, picture how coordinated the caramel blond would look wearing a camel shoe that gives the illusion of being the same color as her hair. Picture the brunette wearing a brown shoe—the same shade of brown as her hair. Then, picture the redhead wearing a rust tone shoe that gives the illusion of being her hair color. Very polished, very balanced, very elegant, very simple.

68

Some "Demystifying" *Smart Tips*

There is an old rule you can follow which is to wear shoes the same color as your hem (skirt, dress, trousers, etc.). This can still work if you want to afford, and can find, shoes in all of the colors this would require.

A more practical, easy guideline is to wear shoes and boots in your hair color and hair highlight color (if it is very apparent), lighter and darker versions of your hair color and your skin tone, depending on how light or dark your outfit. I know, you think I've gone crazy again!

There are two colors that are already part of every outfit you put on—your hair color or hair highlight color (whichever is most visible in all lighting conditions) and your skin tone. These colors are already part of your "color scheme", no matter what, unless you're wearing a hat that totally hides your hair.

Instead of bringing in an "odd" color that doesn't relate to you or the colors in your outfit, bring in one that does. It only makes sense that if you repeat these body colors in accessories (and clothing, too) you will look really *pulled-together*. For example, when you wear a print that has your hair color in it, you look "extra" fabulous!

Match your hair as exactly as possible—in front of a mirror, put the shoe on the floor and glance at yourself to see if it gives the "illusion" of being your hair color or your strong, highly visible, highlights. Redheads and those of you with "silver" (gray) hair, too!

A "short story"…

Many years ago, during a consultation, I was talking to a client about using her hair color (it was brown) as a *basic* shoe color because it would work so well with all of the colors on her chart. She made a "face" and told me that she would never wear brown shoes with navy, for instance. I told her that, of course, navy shoes would be great but asked her (I already knew the answer) why she would never wear brown shoes with navy. She said that she didn't think that navy and brown look good together.

I asked her if she felt she looked good right that minute. She said, "Yes!" I handed her a mirror and asked her to tell me what colors she was wearing. Her medium length brown hair was touching the collar of her *navy* suit—she took one look at the beautiful harmony created by her best brown and navy and immediately got the point. That realization changed her life. By the way, she was wearing black patent shoes.

If your hair color is light and you need a medium or darker-colored shoe, use a camel and brown that are darker versions of your hair color (golden blondes will look for golden camels and golden browns, for example). If you need a light shoe, use your hair color or your skin tone if it is light. If your hair color is medium in tone and you need a darker-toned shoe, use a darker version of your hair color.

Everyone who needs a light-toned shoe can use her skin tone, or a lighter version of her skin tone if it is darker. Light haired women can also use their hair color.

If your hair is very dark brown, you can probably use black when you need a dark shoe (it's a darker version of your hair color)—your mirror will tell you if the color balance is good. If you need a medium or light shoe, use your skin tone and/or lighter or darker versions of your skin tone.

Here are some simple, but so very pulled-together looking, examples of accessorizing a *base* with shoes in your hair color. (For a great look, add a belt that matches your shoes.) The shoe doesn't need to be exact, but it does need to be close enough to give the illusion of being the same color as your hair:

- **Brown hair:** A plum or raspberry base with brown shoes.
- **Blond hair:** A robins-egg blue or turquoise base with camel shoes.
- **Red hair:** A blue-purple base with rust shoes.
- **Black or very dark brown hair:** An emerald green base with black shoes.

Besides having shoes in your hair color, and perhaps your skin tone, you will want to eventually own shoes in any neutral you wear often and in your "core colors". A core color is a favorite color (one that looks great on you, of course) that you wear all of the time. Metallics and "pearlized" finishes that give the illusion of your hair color (bronzes, golds, silvers, and coppers) are also often wonderful choices.

If you plan, and build, your wardrobe around two favorite neutrals and one or two core colors, you can limit the number of pairs of shoes you need to look stylish, allowing you more money (for the budget conscious) to buy better quality or to buy something else you desire. A better quality shoe can upgrade an outfit; an inexpensive shoe can downgrade an outfit.

69

Decisions, Decisions, and More Decisions!

Work to achieve a good "color balance" between your shoe or boot and your attire by using a light or medium tone shoe with lighter colors; a light, medium or dark shoe with medium tone colors (this can depend on the season, how light or dark your hair is and the look you want to create) and medium or dark shoes with darker colors (this can also depend on those things just mentioned).

Great shoe colors to wear with cream or pastel ensembles for a woman that has light to medium toned hair are cream, skin tone, or camel. With medium toned brown or red hair try cream, skin tone, camel, or hair color/hair highlight color. If your hair is very dark brown or black, use cream, skin tone, or black.

One of the most difficult looks to balance is a darker top with a light bottom. You can balance this look by wearing a dark shoe/boot and a dark belt—the belt could have a metallic buckle or some metallic detailing on it.

This look is more easily balanced if there is "less" of the dark top, i.e., short-sleeved/sleeveless/lower neck with skin showing, than when the top has long sleeves. Wearing the top tucked-in is good because less of it shows. Examples:

- Beige trousers with short-sleeved black top (tucked-in) worn with a black belt that has a gold buckle and black shoes.
- A pale pink skirt worn with a charcoal gray long sleeve scoop neck sweater (tucked-in) with a gray belt that has a silver buckle and gray shoes. Add a gray and pink scarf, or pink pearls, and you have even better balance— you now know why.

You can make many combinations work by "bringing the bottom color up" but if you haven't done that, *please* don't wear:

- A light bottom and dark top with a light shoe.
- A medium bottom with a dark top and a light shoe.
- A medium colored dress with a light shoe when your hair is dark.
- A light shoe with a dark outfit.

Your shoe and boot color should always "relate" to your outfit. For example, avoid wearing a red shoe when there is no red anywhere else in your ensemble. A red belt would make the shoe work, but not just red earrings (they are too far apart). What if you carry a red bag? Only if it is with you at all times will it work—at a cocktail party (if you don't lay it down), or out shopping, but not at work because your bag isn't with you any longer once you get through the door.

70

High Gloss Feet

Speaking of the "highest" gloss, if you look great in clear, bright colors, shiny black patent leather will work for you. Those of you who are more enhanced by toned-down colors should avoid solid shiny black patent as the eye can be drawn to the "shine" at your feet.

Patent in toned-down colors and neutrals other than black are fine, as are shoes that are a mix of small amounts of patent (even black if it's one of your best colors) and other materials such as leather, suede, file and canvas. Black patent in small strappy sandals may work, but it's "iffy". You are training your eye, so use your mirror to tell you if the patent still looks *unrelated* to your coloring.

71

Styles Upon Styles!

There are so *many* different shoe styles to choose from—what to do? If you own both your favorite heel height and flats in your hair color, other favored neutrals and your core colors, you will probably have the appropriate shoes for most any attire. The best **basic** (go with anything) heels or flats are cut low in the vamp and fairly low on the sides—giving you a longer leg-line and a less-heavy looking shoe.

Wearing shoes that are too casual, the wrong style, or too heavy for the outfit are often-seen mistakes (matching stockings with shoe color can minimize a heavy looking shoe). When your shoe or boot makes the same statement as your outfit, you are making a statement that you know what's what!

You may wear trendy shoes to work if you are wearing trendy clothing to work, but using a trendy shoe with classic clothing says that you **don't** know what's what. That trendy shoe usually has a specific look it was intended for, and unfortunately, American women have an "unfortunate" tendency to wear/use the latest "in" item with any previously owned item.

So that I only have to "say" it once, instead of a dozen times on the following pages, exceptions are made for trendy, eccentric, and arty dressers!

Using a casual looking shoe with a suit or a heavy looking shoe with a lightweight long skirt also says you don't have a clue. No boots, *please*, with classic suits unless the weather is bad—and then change at the office.

No loafers, oxfords, or other heavy weight shoes with slit skirts. Also, none of these heavy looking styles with knee "hovering" to mid-calf length skirts. Most heavy weight shoes are also too clunky-looking with most long skirts! No matter what the fashion, wearing medium-heavy to heavy looking shoes (especially flats) with below the knee to below mid-calf lengths generally (but not always) gives a dowdy impression.

Open strappy sandals are paired with sundresses, evening dresses (not all of them) and light-weight casual clothing; therefore, they are generally worn during your free time, unless your place of business calls for casual clothing. Under any circumstances, *please* don't wear sandals with any attire that covers up most of your body.

In magazines and catalogues, I've seen many pantsuits shown with sandals (for day and evening wear) and I have to say that it looks really absurd to be **all** covered-up and then have nearly bare feet! The only way to make this look "work" is to:

- Wear a pantsuit that is made out of a light-weight fabric, **AND**

- Leave the jacket open **AND** wear a fairly bare looking top—you need some skin showing to balance the "bare" light-weight looking sandals, **OR**

- If the cut of the jacket allows, wear the jacket buttoned without a top under it—remember, you need to "expose" some skin, but not necessarily cleavage.

Sling backs, or pumps with an open toe, can be worn to work if they make the same statement as your outfit and your outfit makes the right statement for your place of business. Picture a navy sling back or navy pump with an open toe worn in the summer with a short-sleeved light beige silk or rayon suit that is trimmed with navy—beautiful, even for a conservative atmosphere.

No opaque stockings with sandals, sling backs, open toe, or cut out shoe styles, or with short-sleeved or sleeveless tops or dresses, *please*, no matter what you see in the fashion magazines. And, when fall comes, leave "bare" shoes in the closet until the next spring, unless you are wearing them with evening clothes.

Embellished shoes and boots (embroidered, studded, etc.) are wonderful if they go with the look you are creating to further your career—usually more trendy, arty, ethnic, or high-fashion fields. Subtle metallics can be worn in many business environments but shiny metallics are usually best kept for casual day (or evening) looks. You know the exceptions.

Those metallics that are subtle in tone, versus bright and shiny, are best for Gentle and Muted Color Types who are most flattered by toned-down colors. Bright and shiny metallics look wonderful on Contrast and Light-Bright Color Types.

Very sporty looking shoes are only appropriate with casual fabrics and casual attire but a slightly dressier shoe will go with both casual and dressier fabrics and attire. So, if you are on a budget or prefer a minimal wardrobe, which will you buy?

Still getting *smarter*…

If you are on a budget, avoid buying shoes in exaggerated styles. Many will be "out" before you get them broken-in. These styles include: wide square toes, extremely long pointed toes, thick platforms, and very chunky heels.

Shorter boots look best when they fit closely to your ankle and your leg, versus standing-out away from them. Matching stockings that have some weight and/ or texture to the color of your boots helps give the illusion that there is less of a gap.

Shoes and boots with heels covered in the same matching leather are dressier looking than those with heels that are stacked "wood" or a contrasting color.

72

Yikes! More Very Important "Stuff"

What weight shoe looks best with which trouser shape and length? First, you'll need to know which shoe styles are light-weight looking, medium weight looking and heavy looking.

Light-weight shoes include

- Sandals that have very few, light-weight thin straps across the top of the foot;
- Low vamp and low side sling backs;
- Slides/mules with one small, or a few thin straps across the foot;
- All heels, other than flats, will be slim, not chunky; and
- All soles will be thin, not platform.

Please don't ever let your toes hang over the sole of your sandals (or any open toed shoe) or let your heels hang-off the sole in the back. Avoid see-through, plastic sandals and shoes unless you are Cinderella or you are going for a trendy, fashion-forward, or eccentric look.

Medium weight shoes include

- Pumps with a slim heel;
- Low-cut flats with a thin or fairly thin sole;
- Pumps with a high, thicker (but not chunky) heel and a low vamp; and
- Mary Janes and T-straps that have a low vamp, are cut low on the sides, have a slim heel, thin sole, and very narrow, small straps.

Mary Janes, T-straps, and other shoes and sandals with a strap across the instep really shorten your leg line and can make your ankles and calves look thick and/or "sturdy". A shoe or sandal with a strap around your ankle can do the same unless the strap is very fine and the vamp is cut very low. When it comes to any strap across your instep or ankle, it helps lengthen your leg line if your stockings are the same color as your strap.

Medium/Heavy weight shoes include

- Pumps with a medium height, thicker heel;
- Very high-cut pumps with slender heel;
- Some loafers;
- Slides/mules that cover nearly the entire top of your foot;
- Flats that are cut very high in vamp and on the sides; and
- Wedges and platforms usually fall either into this category or the heavy weight category.

Heavy weight shoes include

- Any shoe or sandal (including slides/mules) with a thick/heavy sole, or very chunky heel;
- Most loafers;

- ◆ Oxfords;
- ◆ Athletic shoes;
- ◆ Almost anything with a tongue or laces;
- ◆ Most wedges and platforms with thick soles; and
- ◆ Any shoe or sandal that covers most of the top of your foot.

A high vamp, higher sides, thick/heavy sole, straps across the foot or around the ankle, and a chunky heel can **RAISE** the visual weight of a shoe—so can thicker, courser materials and textures like canvas versus smooth leather. A lower vamp, lower sides, and slimmer heel can **lower** the visual weight of a shoe.

Any light colored shoe with a dark sole or heel looks *heavier* than it would with a matching sole and heel— the exception would be a sole so thin that you didn't even notice it.

Please avoid wearing mules of any style with all covered-up looks. Why? Look at yourself in your mirror from the back (some women think of their full length mirror as a best friend that can't talk back) and you'll see how silly bare heels look when all of the rest of you is covered! Check out sling backs for the same reason.

73

Yes, It's a *Weighty* Subject Matter!

Now, which weight shoe works best with a specific trouser shape and length? Although I'm going to give you a guide, it's not quite that simple because the shoe weight can depend on the weight of the trouser fabric and the occasion.

The lighter the weight and more delicate the fabric, the lighter the shoe needs to be, whatever the trouser style (the same goes for skirts). For example, you know that wider leg trousers are to be worn long, nearly touching the floor in the back with your shoe on. If the trouser is wool, the perfect weight shoe is medium to heavy but never light. But if the fabric is light-weight, like rayon or silk, the shoe shouldn't be any heavier looking than medium weight.

Straight wide leg approximately 10" or more across the bottom

- Any weight shoe/boot or style, depending on fabric.

Straight classic leg approximately 9" across bottom

- Any weight shoe/boot or style, depending on the fabric.

Straight narrow leg approximately 7" across

- Light to medium weight shoe;
- Best with styles that have a low vamp (if fabric is heavier stay with the medium weight shoe); and
- You can also wear a boot that's not too heavy looking.

Very narrow cut (sometimes called cigarette) that are tapered to the ankle and capris

- No heavy weight shoes of any style; and
- Light to medium weight shoe with low vamp (if fabric is heavier, stay with medium weight shoe).

Bell bottoms

- Any weight shoe or boot, depending on the fabric.

Bootleg cut

◆ Medium to heavy weight shoe or boot, depending on the fabric—this cut seems to work best with at least a bit of a heel in a variety of styles. If a so-called "bootleg cut" looks like bell-bottoms, remember: if it walks like a duck and quacks like a duck, it's a duck!

Leggings

◆ Tight to medium weight or tucked into a boot.

Stirrups

◆ Tucked into a boot so the stirrup doesn't show—no exceptions!

As you train your eye to see the best weight of shoe for an outfit, you will also notice that the top/jacket you are wearing with any of these bottoms can affect your choice. Bare or sleeveless tops can call for less weighty looking shoes and "all covered-up" tops/jackets can call for a medium weight shoe instead of a light weight shoe.

From time to time current fashion calls for us to tuck our pants into a boot and that's easy to do when the trouser is narrow—what isn't so easy to do is to wear them over a boot because the taper at the ankle usually makes it impossible to get the bottom of your pants down over the top of your boot. Hence the boot leg cut, slender in the leg but just wide enough at the bottom to fit over boots. No light-weight fabrics with boots, *please*. You know the exceptions.

Shorts

Depending on the look you want to create, you may use any weight shoe with shorter shorts but as the shorts drop in length toward the knee, the shoe weight needs to be medium to light depending on the fabric and some other important details.

One of those details is *what* you are wearing with your shorts. You now understand that sandals and other very light-weight shoes don't work when the rest of you is pretty well covered-up—long sleeves and not much skin showing at the neck. Having bare, or bare-looking legs, doesn't count since all of the "bareness" is at the bottom with none at the top for balance. So, if you are wearing long sleeves and a not very bare top with your shorts, reach for a shoe that is at least medium in weight.

*A little aside...*If you are wearing longer shorts, the width of the legs becomes an important factor to your looking dumpy or stylish. In most instances, you will need to narrow the legs (and sometimes shorten your shorts). Try them on with the shoe you intend to wear them with and, in front of the mirror, pin them in a bit narrower and/or shorten them and check out the difference.

74

Are You Ruining Your Visual Reputation by Wearing "Sneakers" with Your Business Attire? Stop! Don't Do It!! I Won't Even Say *Please*!!!

No exceptions unless your doctor insists that no other shoe made for walking will work for your "problem" (have your problem fixed ASAP). American women are still being laughed at all over the world because of this inappropriate habit. And, if that's not enough to get you to stop doing it, most men would never consider a second look (at least not an admiring look) at a woman who is dressed this way—if you don't believe me, ask them.

For centuries, women have somehow managed to walk long distances without putting on this very clunky-looking footwear. Now, some American women cannot even go out for lunch, or to and from the parking garage, without putting them on.

Several companies make great shoes that are made for walking and/or standing that do not look like athletic shoes. You may not like the way they look with your outfit as well as the shoe you put on when you get to work, but believe me, they will look 1,000 times better than wearing sneakers with your business attire.

75

Never Let a Man, Not Even Your Husband, See You in Knee-Highs or Trouser Socks!

Why? Put them on with just your underlovelies and look in your trusted full-length mirror. Now, take off your underlovelies and look again. Neither image is the least bit sexy— knee-highs are sex-appeal killers! Notice that I'm not asking you not to wear them—I'm just advising that you not get "caught" in them!

Now, I know that there are men who wouldn't/don't care but, these are usually the same men who wouldn't care if your intimate apparel were "underuglies" (perhaps they're in a hurry, or maybe they are just unobservant), and I'm making the assumption that you'd prefer a different kind of guy.

What if you are undressing in front of *him* and what if he's undressing you? It's like choreography—you'll practice to make sure your movements are fluid and natural. If it's you doing the undressing, as you are taking off your trousers, take off one leg at a time, removing that knee-high at the same time. All you have to do is to hook your thumb(s) in the top of them as you are moving down your leg. If he's doing the undressing, you must "help" him when it comes to your trousers, doing it just as described above.

Please, no knee-highs, ever, with a skirt of any length! Yes, someone will know—you.

76

Please Double Check the Color in Natural Daylight!

Have you ever walked out of the house and glanced down at your stockings to find that something's wrong with the color—they don't look the same as they did when you put them on? Natural daylight tells many truths:

- If the color of your foundation is wrong;
- If your makeup is blended well enough;
- If your hair color is flattering to your skin tone;
- If your clothing and accessory colors are working well together; and
- If the color of your stockings is right.

The wrong color of stockings can ruin an otherwise great look. On the other hand, if they are right, you won't notice them except as part of your *Smart* total look.

What could be the matter? Usually:

- Wearing stockings called "suntan" which are most often too dark or reddish.
- Wearing stockings that are too light or too white looking. Often, when stockings are too "white" (even when they may be called bone or ivory), it is because they are too opaque—not sheer enough.
- Wearing stockings that the package said were "off-black"—way off—be aware, some actually have a muddy or green cast!
- Wearing opaque stockings with skirt lengths that hover around the knee.

- Wearing too sheer stockings with very short skirts, definitely a "no, no" for business, *perhaps* okay at a party.
- Wearing patterned or textured stockings when plain would have been more elegant.
- Wearing nude/skin tone stockings when a sheer tint of color or opaque would have been much better.
- Wearing dark stockings when those in a nude/skin tone, or very sheer tint of color, would be more flattering.

Never wear "sun tan" looking stockings unless they are the **exact** color of your skin. They are often too dark and generally too "reddish" or "orangy" looking to have a natural appearance.

A "short-story"

Everyday, during the training of Color 1 Associates, I do a wardrobe critique of each trainee in front of the class. Of course, since they are in training, I don't expect them to know everything when they start so there are usually things that I need to mention.

One particularly stunning and stylish Black "associate to be" came to class the first day wearing black narrow cut trousers, a white blouse, and a black, white, and gray vest with black sling back heels—everything was perfect except for her stockings. Her feet looked "orange"! She went into the ladies room and took off her stockings.

The next day of training, she again came beautifully dressed—this time without stockings, determined not to make the same mistake. The "trouble" was, I had to tell her that she needed to wear stockings that day because she was wearing a classic business look!

Unless you are familiar with the color and the brand, check the color in natural daylight, and check it as well in the same light you work in—lighting can really make colors change drastically and you do not need to start your work day shocked to discover that the color of your stockings is not what you thought.

77

Sheer Decision Making

All women need a sheer nude/skin tone look with certain attire. Check every possible color to find stockings that are perfect for you. Slip one of your arms in the store's sample and hold it up next to your other arm. Your arms should match *exactly*.

When in doubt of what's best, follow these guidelines—there are exceptions, of course, but **most** of the time these *Smart Tips* work great IF you pay attention to your skirt length and the occasion:

- ◆ Wear your nude/skin tone or sheer bone/ ivory with light-colored clothing.

- ◆ With medium colored clothing, wear your nude/skin tone if your shoe is medium in tone; your nude/skin tone or sheer bone/ivory if your shoe is light; and your nude/skin tone (you might be able to use a **very** sheer tint of the shoe color if the shoe is dark).

- ◆ With dark colored clothing, wear a sheer tint of the dark shoe color; a nude/skin tone or a very sheer bone/ivory, depending on the look you'd like, the occasion, the time of year, and the length of your skirt. In the fall and the winter, opaque stockings the color of your shoes (or possibly the color of your skirt or trouser) may be perfect with shorter skirts— it depends on the "depends upon".

- ◆ For a dressier effect, your stockings can be sheerer, especially at night. For example, a short skirt that requires opaque stockings in the daytime can look totally different with sheerer stockings at night.

What in the world could your age have to do with your perfect choice of stockings?

How sheer, medium-opaque, or opaque you wear your stockings is dependent on the look you are creating for your place of business, the length of your skirt, the time of the day or year, the occasion, your shoe style, and your age.

"Age" is mentioned here because short skirts and very short skirts teamed with very sheer stockings can look sleazy instead of sexy on "women of a certain age"—what age is that? You get to pick the number but, if you *feel* uncertain, it's best not to wear this look because the "uncertainty" will keep you from carrying it off. What does shoe style have to do with it? A short skirt worn with sheer stockings and flats, although not conservative, is much more conservative than the same combination with high heels.

Opaque stockings can work well with very long skirts, short skirts, and very short skirts for both day and evening. A slightly opaque look (but not a totally opaque look) is nice with a skirt that is just above the knee. A totally opaque look is often necessary as skirts get shorter in the fall and winter, especially during the daytime.

Skirts that hover around the knee, or fall a few inches below the knee, need very sheer stockings. *Please* avoid wearing opaque stockings with this length skirt.

Very thick stockings (almost as thick as a wool ribbed legging) are for trendy, arty, ethnic, eccentric, or funky looks.

78

Collect All *Data* Before Making a Final Commitment!

It's difficult to make generalizations because the color of stockings, and how sheer or opaque they are, often depends on:

- The weight of the fabric you are wearing;
- Whether your outfit is a light, medium or dark color;
- The time of the day/year;
- The occasion;
- Your Color Type; and
- How much skin is showing or how much is covered-up.

In general, the lighter your hair, the more you will wear nude/skin tone (sometimes sheer bone) and sheer tints of neutrals instead of slightly opaque and opaque stockings. Examples:

- A camel long sleeve top and a black, just above the knee, skirt: use nude/skin tone or **very** sheer black stockings with black shoes. Because your hair is light, if you were to use more opaque black stockings, you could look bottom heavy.
- A navy suit with gold buttons on the jacket and a mid-knee length skirt: stockings can be a very sheer bone, nude/skin tone, or a **very** sheer tint of navy with navy shoes.

Generally, sleeveless and short-sleeved looks are most always appropriate with skin tone/nude stockings. And lighter weight fabrics almost always need sheerer stockings.

It's sometimes difficult to know when to wear pale (nude/skin tone or sheer bone) stockings in the colder months. To help you figure this out, I'm giving you some examples, but I want you to continue training your eye so that when you look at yourself in the mirror you will begin to see the balance between the "uncovered" spaces and the "covered" spaces. When your body is all covered-up (trousers and long sleeves) with mostly dark colors, nude/skin tone stockings can make it look as though you aren't wearing any stockings at all.

Pretend you are wearing the layered look of a cream shirt over a navy wool turtle neck, tucked into navy wool trousers topped with a red wool jacket. The shoe is a navy loafer and the stockings need to be an **opaque** navy—this is a good time to wear opaque navy trouser socks that have a bit of a pattern.

A "short story"...

Most of the time when I'm out and about I am very *unobservant*—I don't "work" by noticing what people are wearing and if it's great or not. I think I'd "burn out" if I did. But once in a while, I'm very "naughty"! On a very cold and blustery New York evening I was having dinner in a famous steakhouse with my best friend, Phyl, and neither of us were paying any attention to anything going on around us. When we're together, we are always brainstorming and planning something to do with our businesses.

Suddenly, I felt someone's eyes on me and I glanced in that direction and met the gaze of a *gorgeous* man. At some time unknown to me, the large round table right next to us had gotten a new group of people—all guys. Exchanging glances once in a while, I couldn't help but notice that he was perfectly, beautifully dressed, except for his socks!

He was wearing a black cashmere turtleneck sweater and heavy black wool cuffed trousers (a black base) and over them, a subtle black and brown plaid wool jacket that had a blue line running through it. His shoes were perfect—brown suede. His socks were very *thin* and "looked" like a creamy white.

Something came over me and I just couldn't help myself. I wrote him a note on the back of one of my business cards that said, "Everything is perfect except for your socks—perhaps you might try blue socks, the shade that's in your jacket." I certainly could have said black or brown socks but I knew that he already knew he could have done that. He was trying for something a touch more avant-garde. As we got up to leave, he said, "Hi." I smiled and handed him my card, which he quickly tucked under his plate—as if none of his guy friends noticed!

Did he call? Because my card reflects the fact that I live in Washington, he didn't have my number in New York. But, just like *magic*, two days later we passed each other on the street (I guess New York is really a small town sometimes) and we couldn't stop to speak because he had "company."

Did he ever call? The next day I was back in Washington and he called. The first words out of his mouth were, "My socks were blue! And I know, they were too pale and too thin!" He's still gorgeous and one of my most adored men friends!

When fabrics are heavier, or you are wearing thicker looking layers, or heavy weight shoes, you need heavier and thicker looking stockings. The opposite is also true, light-weight fabrics call for more sheer stockings. That doesn't mean that there aren't other things to consider. For example:

You're wearing a red wool boucle suit with a just above the knee skirt length. Choices for stockings are: In the fall and winter, a very sheer tint of black or navy (your shoe color) or nude/skin tone. In the spring and summer, if you are a Light-Bright or Gentle Color Type or your hair is light, a nude/skin tone is the best choice and also a good choice for muted and contrast Color Types. What does your Color Type have to do with the color of your stockings or the sheerness of your stockings?

In the fall and winter, if the same red suit skirt is shorter, you can go more opaque—shorter yet, totally opaque, IF you are a Contrast or Muted Color Type with medium dark to dark hair. If your hair is medium or light in tone, a semi-opaque look is dark enough and even then, if you are a Light-Bright or Gentle Color Type, you may need to find a way to lighten up this look. Glance in the mirror: if you look like a "headless person", work your magic. Yes, you do know how: metallic buttons, necklace, and earrings and/or, wear the jacket open with a light top under it—even a belt with a metallic buckle helps!

When you are wearing a longer skirt with a slit, carefully consider if your stockings would be more flattering if they were nude/skin tone (or even sheer bone), a sheer tint of your shoe color, slightly opaque, or totally opaque. Remember your "it depends on" like day or night; dressy, business, or casual; and fabric weight. It also depends on whether your hair is dark, medium, or light in tone, and of course, it depends on the color of the skirt and what you are wearing it with!

There are too many different variants for me to be able to give you specific guidelines so you will have to continue training your eye to see good "balance"—but I will say that if you want to showcase your legs (the reason for the slit?), do not wear totally black opaque stockings with a black skirt, for example, because your legs will get lost.

Avoid wearing opaque stockings in warm weather months. In the spring and summer months your stockings will be lighter, **very** sheer tints of neutrals, nude/skin tone, and sheer bone/ivory. Sheer tints of colors can be used year-round when they are "in" if they work within the parameters of your *career goals*—you know what I mean.

Even when it's very hot outside, go bare legged to work only if your work place is very casual. Even then, if you are wearing attire that calls for stockings, put them on (working and driving in air conditioning takes away any excuse not to wear them).

How do you know if your outfit calls for stockings? If you are wearing pumps (even open toed pumps), or sling backs with a suit, a pantsuit, or a dress that isn't casual, put on stockings. Even many casual dresses look better with stockings. Also, if you are pretty much "all covered-up" (long sleeves, not much skin showing at the neck) bare legs look as totally out of place as sandals. Most of you know, but apparently some of you don't, that when you wear sandals (or any open shoe) you need to wear sandal-foot stockings—no reinforced toes or heels showing, *please.*

If you don't want to wear stockings when it is hot outside, make absolutely certain that your work environment will allow you to wear the type of clothing that goes with a no stocking look. And keep your feet, toe nails, and legs beautifully groomed—no exceptions.

Wear opaque stockings when you are wearing boots with trousers or skirts (exceptions are made for "you know who"). Also make certain that the stockings do not look *thin.* They need enough visual weight to look good with the weight of the boots. How would anyone know what stockings you are wearing with your boots and trousers? When you sit down and cross your legs, your stockings often show—this is a good time to add a touch of *style* with patterned knee highs!

79

The *Allure,* or Possible *Horror,* of Patterns and Textures

Stockings that have visible texture and patterns come and go in fashion and are definitely more appropriate with high fashion, trendy, funky, eccentric, arty, romantic, or ethnic looks than they are with classic looks. You can try the more *subtle* patterns with long skirts or trousers—if you have any doubts for your work place, restraint is advised.

For those of you who can dress more trendy or funky at work, try them with shorter skirts. Remember, within certain guidelines, the shorter the skirt, the more opaque the stockings. Why am I pointing this out again? Because not all textures and patterns are "opaque"—many have a lot of open work. So, with shorter skirts, open textures become more appropriate for evening than daytime.

When wearing textured and patterned stockings it's best to keep everything else plain and simple—it's easy to look overdone. Small, subtle patterns can be worn more successfully than those that are medium and large in scale. For example, the "Swiss-dot" (sheer tint of neutral with matching dot, like sheer black with a tiny black dot or sheer bone with a tiny bone dot) is the most conservative pattern, and when "in style", can be worn with femininely styled suits and dresses.

The very best way to wear textured and patterned stockings with classic styles is to pair them with pantsuits and trousers—just a touch of texture or pattern showing at the ankle adds style and interest. It might even say, "This is an interesting woman."

80

"Color" Down There?

Stockings in colors like blue, purple, or red come and go in fashion and are still "suspect" in several business fields.

For the adventuresome who can wear colors to work, some great looks are created by:

+ Wearing a totally all one color look from shoe to earrings (everything red, for example);
+ Putting together a monochromatic color scheme with lighter and darker tones of the

same color, like mixing beige, camel, medium brown, and dark brown; or light purple, medium purple, and dark purple; and

- Definitely not for most workplaces, by "color blocking"—using two or more blocks of colors like black shoes, red opaque stockings, short black skirt, and a red top.

81

No "Baggy" Stockings, Please!

Stockings that are too big for you, or that are very sheer, can "bag" at the ankles and knees. For all pantyhose, try to find a size where your weight and height fall in the middle of the chart, not right on the edge where you are close to needing a smaller size or larger size.

If you do end up on the "edge", consider the size and length of your legs. For example, I'm 5' 8½" tall and my legs are short (for my height), and although not skinny, they are slim. So if I'm on an edge where I'm wondering if I should buy the larger size or the smaller size, I buy the smaller.

Having even a hint of lycra in your stockings (often called lycra sheers) helps keep them from bagging and helps them wear longer, making them one of the best choices for work.

82

Keep a "Spare Pair" Handy!

Keep an extra pair of your most used neutrals at work and NEVER run out at home. Change the minute you get a visible run or hole. Don't start the day with stockings that have several visible snags, you won't feel you look your best and it will affect your entire day. Save snagged stockings to wear under trousers or long skirts with boots.

83

What's in Your Sock Drawer?

No socks with sandals unless you are eccentric (or creating a trendy, funky look). Wearing shoes with "socks" that *show* skin above them, other than for athletics or with casual shorts, is a fad unless you are 10-years-old or younger—I just picked ten arbitrarily because if I were 11, I think I'd want to start dressing more like I was 12, which, after all, is nearly a teenager!

What do I mean by shoes with socks that show skin above them? A "classic" look for many women is jeans or casual pants worn with socks and loafers. It's best that you aren't able to see your bare leg above your socks, even when you are seated and cross your legs. If you are wearing athletic shoes with jeans or casual pants, the same applies. That means no short, just above the shoe, socks for anything but athletics. Even then, classic socks that you fold down look better than short, ankle socks. Don't believe me? Do a mirror test. The sock that you fold down creates a better "transition" between your leg and big, heavy looking athletic shoes.

84

Going Casual

American casual wear is world renowned for its style—our U.S. designers and manufacturers do it better than anybody! Why, then, do so many American women look unstylish in their casual clothes when we have so many great styles to choose from? Part of the reason is right there—there are *soooooo* many styles to choose from!

Never fear, you've been training your eye and every *Smart Tip* you have been reading and practicing can be applied to casual attire. All of the principles are the same, only the fabrics and detailing may be more casual.

Another "part of the reason" for looking unstylish is that some women seem to think or feel that casual, grubby, and sloppy are synonyms.

Think casual elegance! *Yikes,* am I telling you that you need to dress-up all of the time? No, only that I want you to look as great in your jeans and T-shirts as you do at work or at a party. It's all a matter of *Dressing Smart* and looking "pulled-together".

I'm writing this portion of **Dressing Smart...** on China Beach in Vietnam. It's a "long story", but basically I'm in Vietnam because a very *smart* and stylish Vietnamese woman is interested in having me train some Color 1 International Image and Style Consultants here.

As the country "emerges", many jobs are being created for women; although they wear their traditional dress so beautifully, they are starting to dress more and more in the type of clothing we wear in the States. Just like women everywhere, without *Smart Lessons* they don't know how to put clothing pieces together to create a stylish, well-coordinated appearance.

For example, you'll see a young woman wearing a bold black and white striped sweater with a delicate floral patterned pastel peach and yellow skirt. She doesn't know that they don't look good together.

I'm also here to shop! But, this time, it's part of my job to shop!! Really!!! I'm going to advise two very forward-thinking women (both own travel agencies, one in the States and one in Vietnam—the same chic woman I just mentioned) who are developing shopping tours to Vietnam.

If you are interested in finding out more about this remarkable shopping experience, check the Resource Center—you might be interested in seeing Vietnam with an image consultant who will make sure that you return home with several "million dollar looks".

As I'm sitting here barely able to keep my eyes off the South China Sea, I can't help but notice that the American, Eastern European, Australian, and some of the Japanese tourists look like, horrors, "tourists"—

sloppy and poorly dressed! There is no reason why you can't look great in your casual attire and feel comfortable, too, whether you are traveling, shopping or just *hanging-out.*

85

Working with a Casual *Base*

One of the ways to simplify your casual life and look stylish at the same time is to wear *bases*. If the clothing you choose to assemble these bases is comfortable (loose fitting, breathes, and perhaps has some give), you will be too! If you need warmth, or a different look, top your base with another layer (jacket, sweater, shirt, or vest). Use your hair color (or a lighter or darker version of your hair color) for shoes/sandals, belt, and bag. Can't find your hair color, or even the illusion of it? Keep looking, and meanwhile, use another one of your best neutrals or a metallic.

For wonderful casual summer looks (day or night), use a metallic belt with your base and matching metallic shoes. Of course, your hair colors or another best neutral can be substituted. Here are some examples:

- Cream pants and matching sleeveless top with a gold metallic belt and gold flats or sandals.
- Green cotton shorts with a matching short-sleeved T-shirt, with a copper belt and copper sandals—yes, a **base** with shorts is fabulous looking!
- Coral skirt and a matching tank worn with a silver belt and silver low-cut flats.
- Blue jeans shirt (sleeves rolled up)with blue jeans, copper metallic belt, and flats or sandals.

In the fall and winter seasons, you can substitute hair colors and other best neutrals for the metallics, change the shorts to pants and the sleeveless and short-sleeved tops to long-sleeved tops or sweaters.

Of course, you can use *your* favorite colors instead of these and you can dress these looks "up" in the summer by doing them in washable silks, rayons, and linens and in the winter by using any warmer fabric that you love. Don't forget to use flats instead of sandals if you are wearing long sleeves, unless you push or roll up your sleeves or your top is cut with lots of skin showing! I'm sure you know to let the sandals have a vacation during cool and cold weather months.

86

Moms Can Be Really "Neat" and Interesting Women, Too...

Some women wonder why their significant other takes them for granted and why there seems to be a "respect" issue with the children. Often, your younger significant others don't have a clue as to "who" you really are, how very good you are at your job, and how admired you are by others. They probably think that you're a special "mom"—but they don't know that you are a special *person*! They just think of you as mom, instead of a *really neat lady*. Perhaps "he" thinks the same. Could it be because most of the time you spend with them, your image is less than wonderful? Less than good? Less than okay?

Knits, micro fibers, and anything with *stretch*, especially those that are washable, are the answers to great looking, **comfortable**, casual clothing! And they take away any excuse for not looking great ALL OF THE TIME!! *Please* toss your "grubbies" so you won't be tempted to wear them ever again!!!

Great casual looks include super tops and sweaters (always keep your eye out for great looking tops) worn with jeans and pants made in fabrics that have some lycra or spandex in them. Try the stretch-enhanced cotton, corduroy, denim, velvet/velveteen, and other fabrics that include these miracle fibers.

"Casual comfort" includes pants and skirts that have elastic waist bands—there is absolutely nothing wrong with this "as long as" you can't see the waist band. All you have to do is wear your top out—it has to be a super looking top, not one that looks sloppy.

There are some great dresses, both short and long, that you can just pull-on and wear with a pair of sandals in the summer—the long-sleeved, warmer winter version of this dress is worn with comfortable boots or shoes. Depending on your climate and the fabric of the dress, you may be able to layer long sleeves under a "summer" dress to create a "winter", or maybe just a "fall", dress.

When you come home from work in the summer, nothing could be easier, more comfortable, or more alluring than slipping on a slip dress, a tank style, or something similar! In the winter, consider pulling-on narrow leg pants that fit well but have a lot of *give* and topping them with a color-perfect, easy-fitting sweater in chenille, perhaps.

87

Carrying a *Smart* Bag

If everything looks great but your bag, do you look great? Elegant? Stylish? **NO!** Carrying the wrong bag can ruin your look. No matter how much else you've done right, the wrong bag (including your briefcase and your luggage) sends a message to the contrary!

In years past, our bag had to match our shoes. Now it is acceptable for them to be different—both just have to go with our outfit. Actually, following the old rule is easy and "well pulled-together looking". I highly recommend it because it keeps women from reaching for an *odd* bag that they may think works fine when it really doesn't.

88

The Most *Versatile* Bags

A bag in your hair color and/or highly visible hair highlight color is a great choice because it's always part of your color scheme—remember, unless your hair is totally hidden by a hat, it is part of every look you create. *Please* explore the first few paragraphs of your *Smart Tips* for shoes and boots if you do not, yet, understand this concept.

Other excellent, possible colors: lighter and darker versions of your hair colors, your skin tone (again, always part of every color scheme you create), all neutrals you wear often and your core colors. Just as with shoes, Gentle and Muted Color Types should avoid solid black patent.

Metallics are most often used for evening or for daytime casual, but can be used for daytime business if your "business" look calls for a metallic bag.

Bags with two-tone patterns only look great with an outfit in those exact colors. Likewise, bags with logos all over them only coordinate well with something in the same color(s).

89

Your Bag Needs to Make the Same "Statement" as Your Ensemble...

Here are some examples that DON'T

- ◆ A trendy or fashiony looking bag with classic clothing like a fringed suede pouch or a backpack with a classic suit;

- ◆ A structured, heavy looking leather shoulderbag with a feminine, elegant linen silk suit;

- ◆ A delicate-looking skin bag with a wool plaid suit; and

◆ A classic tailored suit bag with a trendy/funky look.

Backpacks are "classic" for students and backpacking only. They can also be quite helpful for moms with babies and toddlers. A few years ago, backpacks made mostly in leather and nylon became "fashionable" for daily use when they were carried over one shoulder, not both. No matter how beautiful and stylish, they are more appropriate with casual and trendy attire than they are with classic business looks.

90

Buy the *Basics* First

Let's just suppose that you don't own even one bag, what would you buy first? A bag in your most used neutral without embellishment, or any metallic hardware showing, is a great *Smart Basic* because it works beautifully with so many different outfits. Whether your other accessories and buttons are gold, silver, pearls, etc., this bag will look good! If you lost all of your bags, this should be the first bag you buy.

Can't find a "plain" one you like? Keep looking and meanwhile, if you wear both gold and silver jewelry, you will need one bag that has gold detailing and one that has silver.

Always coordinate any metallic color on a bag or tote with your jewelry, buttons, and buckle. For example, *please* do not carry a bag that has gold "hardware" when you are wearing silver earrings.

"Collect" small plain bags because they go with a greater variety of ensembles. If you avoid sporty leathers, sporty detailing and sporty clasps, you have a bag that you can carry with a business look, some evening looks (not black tie) and sporty looks as well.

How small is *small?* Certainly, it depends somewhat on the shape/style of the bag, but I'm giving you measurements, not because I want you to grab a ruler and measure your bags but because most of you are thinking that a bag is small when it's actually medium size or larger!

Depending on its shape, a small bag is **approximately** 7" by 10", 8" by 8", or smaller; Medium is around 8" by 11"; and large is almost anything larger than medium. Any bag that is "thick" (front to back) gives a larger look. And if you "stuff" any bag so it bulges, it obviously looks larger than it is and it looks inelegant. Very structured bags can look larger than bags with softer lines.

Let's say that you have a date right after work and you walk into the restaurant carrying a large bag or a tote. I don't think that you want him (or anyone else) to think that you're planning to spend the night! Having a small bag tucked into a tote allows you to check your tote and bring your small bag to the table. If you are carrying a briefcase, no problem, but I'd still check it so you won't be reminded of work while you're having dinner.

91

Carry the Right Size of Bag for Your Coloring. I Know, Crazy Lady!

If you have delicate coloring, a medium size bag *looks* larger when you carry it than when a person with strong coloring is carrying it. If you carry a large bag it can look like you're carrying a tote. Unless you are going for the look of a tote, stay with small and medium sized bags.

If you have strong coloring, you can carry a bag of any size; however, when it comes to large bags, petites need to judge whether the bag looks like a purse or a tote.

Does your height have an effect? Yes it can, but if your coloring is delicate, being taller doesn't mean you can go much larger without having your bag look overwhelming. Delicate coloring is most enhanced by creating a delicate look in clothing and accessories. A large bag just doesn't look delicate. Don't believe me? Ask your mirror!

92

Now's Not the Time to Get *Lazy*!

Get in the good habit of emptying your bag into a lovely tray or basket at the end of each day (like a man empties his pockets—he could have his own tray). The next day, that will "force" you to reach for a bag that compliments your attire and fill it with only those things you need—remember, an overstuffed bag does not look *Smart*.

Too much work? Won't do it? Then only wear outfits that look great with the one bag you are willing to carry every day! No, no exceptions.

93

No Bags in Need of Repair, *Please*

Just as with shoes, a quality bag can upgrade your ensemble; an inexpensive bag, or a bag in need of repair, can downgrade your look! No "plastic" or faux leather bags—you can buy quality leather goods on sale or at discount stores.

94

Toting in Style

Carry a briefcase or tote in your most used neutral or your hair color. If your hair is light, use a darker version of the same color—if you are a golden blond, for instance, use a golden camel or a golden brown. If you can afford more than one briefcase or tote, add another in your second most used neutral.

I recommend less "mannish" looking briefcases—those that look less structured. Also, buy the best quality you can afford and then carry it *forever*. This will be one of your best investments because it's part of your first and last impression!

Please don't carry a large bag or tote at the same time you are carrying a briefcase unless you're headed for a plane or train. A smaller bag (I recommend a shoulder-bag) can be carried with a briefcase without making you look like a pack mule. Ideally, if you carry a small bag, it would fit inside your briefcase—in a "perfect" world. *Please* do not ever carry bags over both shoulders.

With suits and business dresses, no casual canvas totes unless you are on your way to the gym—even then, I'd really like for you to invest in a "gym" bag that has a bit of elegance because you will be seen with it several times a week. Since my wish for you is that you always look stylish, I don't want a bag to detract from your look, especially one that you carry so often. Trust me, it's worth the investment!

95

YIKES! Belly Bags and Fanny Packs

Suddenly I'm at a loss for words! I just keep shaking my head and I don't want to write about this subject. I know that these bags are "useful" at times but when worn for other than athletics, they make the wearer look unsophisticated. What about for travel? I wouldn't if I were you—travelers fared just fine for the many years before these bags came into "fashion". If you want your hands free, wear a shoulder-bag across your body.

Okay, just a few more words: belly bags and fanny packs look just a *tiny* bit better on men; those that are smaller look a whole lot better than those that are larger; when they are worn "off-center" they are a hint less horrid than when they are worn right smack on your belly. Their newest incarnation (a fad), sometimes called hands free bags, hipster bags, hip bags, or body pouches are certainly more feminine in the smallest size, looking more like a decorated bag on a belt. They rarely look good on an outfit and they create many line and design concerns.

96
Every One of You Can Look Great in Belts

Opening with a controversial statement is supposed to get your attention!

Do I have it? Good!! You can ask any *sane* woman or man if she/he thinks that all women can wear belts and look great and they will tell you, "NO WAY!!!"

It all has to do with the *way* a belt is worn. Let's start right off with an example so I'll have your trust once more. The woman in this example is a Contrast Color Type, probably a size 22, but she could be a 14, 16, 18, 20, or 24. She is wearing a bright blue *base* and a fairly wide great looking black and gold belt which she has been careful not to belt too tightly because she doesn't want the belt to "ride-up" on her tummy. She has purposefully placed this belt where her "natural" waistline would be if it weren't for her tummy.

On top of this base with its belt, she is wearing a simple black cardigan style jacket that hangs open (in a straight vertical line) so that several inches of the belt shows. When you look at her in this outfit, her waist only looks as wide as the part of the belt that's visible! In fact, without the belt her waist looks *bigger*. **Seeing is believing!**

Hopefully having won back your trust, here's more "stuff" about belts. Own *basic* and "statement" belts (if you love them) in your most used neutrals, your hair color, your core colors, and your best metallics. It's super to have belts in all of the colors that you use for shoes and boots because it makes coordination so very easy!

Purchase first very plain belts with just simple, but elegant, buckles. They are so basic that they can be worn with many different looks without greatly interfering with buttons on jackets and earrings and necklaces.

One and one-half inches is a good *classic* belt width because it fits through most belt loops. By the way, if you don't want to always have to wear a belt, carefully remove belt loops!

97

What's Small Can Look Medium and Vice Versa; and What's Medium Can Look Wide and Vice Versa!

Every one of you can wear a wide belt—another crazy statement, you say. It all depends on *how wide* is wide for you without being overly wide, and it depends on "how" you wear it. What looks wide on me may look overly wide on you and what looks narrow on me may look more medium sized on you.

Your "coloring" comes into play as well, as those of you with delicate coloring should avoid heavy looking belts whatever their size. Also be aware that "medium" size belts could look wide on you (but perhaps not too wide).

Whatever your height or weight, if you have a lot of space between your waist and bosom, you usually have the choice of wearing a belt at your natural waistline, or more loosely, letting it "sling" or angle, down lower on your hips.

If you have little space between your waist and bosom, you can use the same belt but you will want to wear it lower (try "anchoring" it on one side at the waist and angling it down toward the opposite hipbone). A narrower belt at the waist will also work well. Just avoid wearing your belts too close to your bosom because it can make you look saggy, droopy, or dumpy—*yikes!* Who wants that?

A "tummy" can cause a belt to ride-up in the front, creating the illusion that your bosom is lower and making your tummy look more prominent. Angling your belt, as above, always gives a better result but sometimes all you need to do is to loosen your belt and "blouse" your top a little. How? Once your top is tucked in, raise/shrug your shoulders and this can elongate your top just enough to give you good balance. Need more? Angle your belt and blouse your top.

98

Matching Metallics, Again...

Consider the metal color of your buckles. Lets say that navy is a basic neutral for you, and you love both gold and silver jewelry. Unless you can find a navy belt with a covered navy buckle (no metallic showing anywhere) you will need two navy belts—one with a gold buckle and one with a silver buckle.

Also consider metallic buttons when you put on a belt—gold buttons with gold belt buckles, silver with silver, bronze with bronze and copper with copper.

99

Embellish Away!

Embellished belts and arty and ethnic belts are fabulous with certain attire. For some women they are a "signature statement" and they can be worn to work if your position allows clothing that calls for them.

Crystals on a belt make it more for evening or day and evening for more fashiony/funky dressers than a belt with gold or silver studs. A belt with metallic studs can be worn to almost any place of business, depending on what you are wearing it with. Although both are "decorative", a Chanel style chain belt is more classic (and therefore appropriate for classic, but stylish, business attire) than a belt that mixes leather, reptile skin, suede, crystals, and studs.

Sometimes a stunning belt need be the only focal point of your outfit for the work place—a single major statement is enough; adding "major" statement earrings would be *too much*. Your earrings must still make the same statement as your belt, just one that is more subtle.

100
Getting *Smarter*, Still...

If you're wearing a belt on top of a patterned garment, make certain that the color of the belt is highly visible in the print. Look in your full-length mirror from a few paces away. If you can't see the belt color in the pattern, you'll want to change to a belt that looks related from a distance, not just from close-up.

Make sure that your belt style and/or buckle style aren't "fighting with" the style of your outfit or any other accessory you are wearing including your necklace, earrings and any buttons. Examples of incompatibility are a contemporary rectangular shaped buckle worn with dainty filigreed round earrings; a trendy belt with a classic business suit; or a structured belt with a femininely-styled dress made of a light weight fabric.

Please do not place a belt on a top that has ribbing around the bottom. Most jackets and blazers should never be belted; and *please* do not belt anything with pocket flaps or patch pockets that fall below the belt unless you are creating a safari look. Often, what you choose to "leave off" is as important as what you add. There are very rare exceptions here, so let your mirror guide you if you are tempted to try this look.

101
Your Earrings—Placing a Spotlight on Your Face

Yes, earrings do call attention to your face, not a bad thing at all as long as the glances are admiring!

How important are earrings? Well, let's just say that since they can make us look silly or stylish, like we need a face lift (when, perhaps, we've already had one) or like we've had one (when we haven't), they are very significant!

That doesn't mean that you always have to wear them; as a matter of fact, sometimes the best move you could make would be to reach up and take them off! When? When you don't have the appropriate earrings or when wearing them gives you a more "dressed-up" look than you want.

It is important to wear earrings that work (from a statement, style and color standpoint), with your outfit *and* your face shape.

- Pair classic understated earrings, instead of "dangle", ethnic or glitzy earrings, with classic suits and business dresses.
- Wear funky earrings with "far-out" looks instead of a classic small gold knot. And
- Marry wearable art earrings with arty or more casual looks instead of wearing them with a business suit.

Make certain that the style and shape of your earrings are compatible with any buttons on your jacket or top. For example, delicate pink and ivory cameo earrings will not enhance a pink suit that has gold geometric buttons. Obviously, necklaces and earrings must also work very well together, and with your ensemble. If your earrings go well with your outfit, and your outfit is appropriate for your work, your earrings will be as well.

102

Getting Even *Smarter*, Yet...

Earrings that looks large on one woman will look medium sized on the next and vice versa—it depends on the size of your head, your hair style and your coloring. Yes, I know you think I'm crazy, but the size of your earring and your coloring are related.

If you have more delicate coloring, avoid large earrings (unless they are very lightweight looking) because they can easily look "overdone" on you. On the other hand, if your coloring is stronger, small earrings can look insignificant.

Also, pay attention to your hair style. If you wear your hair pulled back, or if it's cut quite short so that your ears totally show, earrings may be more important in achieving a finished, balanced look. But, beware (be aware) that larger earrings tend to "standout" if you are wearing your hair in these styles because the *entire* earring shows. If your hair is styled in such a way that it covers part of your earring, a larger earring can look more subtle.

Position clip earrings so that they rest right next to your face—this way they won't "flop" around when you move your head. Instead of clipping them on your ear lobe, clip them in the space where your lobe meets your face.

103

Focusing on the Ears and Eyes

If you wear glasses, finding the perfect earrings is a bit more difficult. Keeping your glasses free of embellishment and very simple (do not read boring, read: elegant) helps. If your glasses have metallic frames, your earrings need to be the same metallic. So, if you love gold and silver jewelry, you will need two pairs of glasses or one pair that combines gold and silver.

If your glasses do make a statement of any kind, your earrings must make the same! For example, glasses that have "dainty" detailing are not compatible with earrings that have a modern design or a funky/trendy look. For more about glasses, see *Smart Tip* #117.

104

More Matching Metallics

If your jacket buttons or belt buckle are gold, use gold at your ear; if silver, use silver, and so on. Metallic colors can be mixed *if* the mix is carried out as a "color scheme"—mix your metallics on purpose! If a necklace combines silver and gold (or you twist a silver necklace and a gold necklace together), the earrings can be either one of those metallics as can your jacket buttons, bracelet, and belt buckle.

Owning earrings that combine your favorite metallics is helpful. If your earrings are a color, make certain that the same color is apparent in your attire from a few paces away, not just up close.

105

Selecting Great Shapes

What about your face shape with certain styles of earrings? It used to be that women wanted to avoid wearing earrings that repeated their face shape, unless their face was "oval". Now that women are *finally* beginning to understand that there are vast variations on what's considered attractive—this makes them more likely to "play-up" their face shape than try to change it with *illusion*.

The one exception I see is a very long face, especially when it is attached to a long, slender neck. Dangle or drop earrings can make the face and neck appear even longer, depending on what you are wearing. If you are wearing a turtle neck, or are standing up your collar, you may love the effect of long earrings especially if they have "weight" (substance) up on your ear, before the "drop" starts (picture at least medium size earrings covering part of your ear with a drop/dangle attached).

Again, your hair style can come into play here because if you are wearing it in a style that makes your face look **broader**, you may have created enough "balance" (the illusion of width) to counteract the increased illusion of length created by long earrings.

106

Wrapped in Romance—the Necklace

Whether it's an old fashioned choker, a turquoise and silver squash blossom, or a tiny cord with a little pendant, there is something so romantic about necklaces. Unfortunately, like hats, necklaces are items women buy but seldom wear, although they may wear their one or two favorites all the time even if they don't really enhance an outfit. Here are some *Smart Tips*:

♦ A good simple rule is to have your necklace follow the same shape (or line) as the neckline of your outfit. Wearing a necklace that hangs in a "V" shape with a rounded or jewel neckline is an example of incompatible lines.

♦ If you would like a necklace that normally hangs in a "round" shape to work well with a "V" shape neckline, try hanging a pendant, or pin, on it. Hanging pins on your necklaces can create some fantastic looks!

♦ When in doubt, under-accessorize.

♦ If your place of business calls for clothing that may call for an ornate or glitzy necklace, then wearing one is not a mistake for you as long as you still look elegant.

♦ Glitzy and ornate necklaces are not part of classic business attire but if you love them, and can't wear them to work, you can enjoy them in your free time.

♦ If you need to dress more conservatively at work but still would really love to "do more", try wearing a collection of simple, small necklaces, like a few strands of pearls and small gold chains together—add pearl and gold earrings. Or

◆ Wear a larger pendant (or pin) on one strand of pearls or one simple chain and keep your earrings simple.

When a necklace falls partially on bare skin and partially on your top, there is probably a better choice. Experiment by holding your necklace shorter, so that all of it falls on bare skin, and by dropping it lower, so that it falls on your top. You can shorten your necklaces—if your hair hangs down over the clasp in the back, simply tie a knot before you fasten it around your neck (sometimes a knot that shows in the front is nice, too). Your jewelry store may carry necklace extenders and shorteners.

107

Getting the Scale Right for Your "Coloring"

I know it sounds crazy, but if your coloring is delicate, wear small and medium sized necklaces, avoiding large scale designs unless they are very lightweight looking. If your coloring is stronger, wear medium and larger scale designs, avoiding small pieces—they can look totally insignificant on you unless you strengthen their look by combining them in a "collection".

To increase the size of a necklace, you can wear several together—try twisting a strand of pearls with a gold and/or silver chain (get daring and twist into those a strand of turquoise or coral). Need more? Knot them all together and let the knot show. If your coloring is delicate, you can do the same as long as you don't create something that is too large or bulky looking.

108

Getting "Colorful"

What about "right and wrong" when it comes to color in necklaces? There are two types of wrong. The first is wearing a color that doesn't enhance your attire. The second is wearing a color that doesn't enhance you!

To make certain the color of your necklace works well with your outfit, the color needs to be repeated at least once somewhere: in a print, the skirt/trouser color, the top color or the belt color (but not just the shoe color). Make sure that you can see the relationship of the colors from a few steps away. As far as the other "wrong" goes, if the colors in your outfit are great on you, the necklace color will be as well!

109

All That *Glitters* Isn't Gold!

Everyone can wear both gold and silver. If you look best in clear, vibrant colors, avoid wearing dull, tarnished metals. If you are more enhanced by toned-down, muted looking colors, avoid large amounts of bright, shiny metals.

Your metallic colors need to look great together, too. For example, gold buttons on a jacket require the same *shade* of gold in earrings and/or necklace—not one that appears more yellowish, pinkish, or brassy.

110

Making the Same Statement Is as "Critical" As Ever!

Avoid wearing:

◆ A tailored gold necklace with a floral print;

- ◆ A necklace with rounded beads with a geometric print;
- ◆ A trendy fashion-forward necklace with a conservative dress;
- ◆ Some ethnic necklaces with classic suits—it depends on the necklace, of course, and it's difficult to tell you which may work without seeing them. An example of one that wouldn't work would be a delicate necklace of beads and feathers worn with a suit that has severe or crisp tailoring. An example of an ethnic necklace that would work is a more tailored looking inlaid turquoise and silver necklace that just circles the base of the neck worn with a gray suit that has a jewel neckline.

If you are not certain that an accessory is "additive", leave it off. Remember that your necklace and earrings must look great together **and** with your attire.

Two of the most common mistakes women make is wearing a small gold chain or a strand of pearls with everything—often a gift from a loved-one whom they wish to honor by wearing it all of the time. If it doesn't *add* style to your look, it may be taking some away! If you don't wish to break a *bond,* carry your loved-one's gift with you in your bag (protected in a small pouch or box).

I think the idea of wearing a strand of pearls with everything is a throwback to the days when mothers told daughters that, "A strand of pearls is always appropriate." Actually, at that time, they pretty much were because clothing choices were more limited. Remember the twin-sets with the pearl, or pearlized buttons? A great classic look with a strand of pearls for yesterday, and a "pushed to the forefront of fashion" look for today!

"Pearls" come in many different colors, including many shades of white, cream, and even a *champagne* color. If you are wearing beige or camel on the "bottom" and need to bring that color "up", champagne or beige toned pearls work beautifully. You can use a gold necklace to do the same—but a tiny chain isn't enough to do it! Do a "mirror test" to check for the needed balance. Use gray pearls and silver necklaces to balance gray.

111

Your Grandmother or Great-Grandmother Probably Wouldn't Have Felt "Dressed" Without a Pin

They are wonderful if you can figure out exactly where to place them, and if they work in harmony with the style and shape of your garment and your other accessories, buttons, and buckles. It's really difficult to get it right, but when you do it's marvelous and fun! Examples to **avoid**:

- A square pin placed on a rounded or shawl collar (like shapes compliment each other);
- A pearl pin on a jacket with gold buttons (a pin that combined pearls and gold would be great);
- A delicate floral pin with a tailored chain choker (accessories need to make matching statements—you can wear the pin without the necklace or, if the pin has a touch of gold in it, try hanging it on a more delicate chain, or grouping of chains, to give a pendant effect); and
- Avoid using pins to "bring the bottom color up"—they are usually not large enough to give you the visual balance you'll need.

It's really fun to place a pin on a necklace—just thread it through a chain or carefully pin it between beads or links. You can get a pendant effect by hanging it on the bottom of the necklace, but you can also pinch the necklace together right at the base of your neck, putting the pin through/around both sides to create a "bolo" effect. You can do the same at any place between the base of your neck and the bottom of the necklace—whatever effect looks best with your neckline.

112

Big, Brilliant, Subtle, Heirloom, Ethnic or Modern, Do You Look Like "a Million Dollars" If You Wear Several Rings at the Same Time?

How many rings can you wear and still look elegant? The answer depends on whom you ask. One of my elegant male friends isn't even interested in meeting a beautiful woman if she is wearing more than one ring (total). Another of my elegant male friends is perfectly charmed by women who wear more than one ring, even on the same hand.

My advice for most women is that *less is more* but your particular *style* may say more is better—you must decide for yourself. Should you decide to wear more than one, make absolutely certain that the rings compliment each other in style and color as well as compliment your other accessories, including buttons and buckles.

A ring (one only) that is quite large, or large looking on your hand, makes an "unusual" statement, usually too much so for many places of business. If you can wear arty, ethnic, funky, or trendy looks to work, great! If not, wear your larger rings in your free time. The same applies for trendy, or "far-out" looking rings.

If you wear a wedding ring that has a diamond(s) set in gold, you may wear it with both gold and silver earrings, necklaces, pins, bracelets, watches, buttons, and buckles because the ring gives both a gold and "silver" look.

If you wear a ring that has a diamond(s) set in platinum or white gold, it goes best with just silver accessories, buttons, and buckles. But wait! You can wear it with gold jewelry, too. How? There are two ways. You can add small (yellow) gold "guard" rings on either side of your ring; or you can wear both a (yellow) gold bracelet and a silver bracelet on the same side you wear your ring.

113

From the Finely Crafted Ethnic to the Museum Quality Keepsake, Bracelets Are Splendid!

But bracelets that clatter, tinkle, or clunk can give your co-workers a splendid headache, or just be a terrible irritant or distraction. So unless you work alone, no bracelet noise, *please.*

Three small, simple bracelets worn together can look more conservative than one large embellished cuff. Several smaller bracelets stacked up the arm look great with an ensemble that calls for them, just as glitzy, ethnic, or other specifically styled bracelets may be worn with outfits that they enhance. Just make certain that the look you are creating makes the statement that you wish to make at *your* place of business.

Avoid wearing bracelets that compete in style and/ or color with each other, or with your other accessories, especially your rings, your buttons, and belt buckle.

Bracelets that hang down over your hand are fine UNLESS they hang so low that they look like they are about to fall-off!

114

From Timeless Elegance to Sporty Chic—Your Watch

Some women have been inspired to start collecting watches because they have finally realized that one watch just won't work with everything, and besides, it's fun! You don't have to collect them but you do need to consider them, just as you would your other jewelry, in the overall look you are creating. Here are some of the most common mistakes that women make with their watches:

- Wearing a watch that doesn't make the same statement as your outfit like a sporty look with business attire;

- Wearing one that has a band in a color that doesn't go with your attire or look good with your skin tone;

- Wearing a gold watch when you are wearing silver jewelry or vice versa—"collect" one that combines both gold and silver; and

- Wearing a watch that has a face that is too white for your skin tone—it will look inexpensive on you if you are a Gentle or Muted Color Type. The white will be the first thing your eye goes to when you glance at it—an off-white or cream face will be so much richer looking.

You can always keep your watch in your bag if it isn't "additive" to your look. I happen to love to wear men's watches so I don't have any delicate looking styles (my coloring is strong, so "dainty" styles don't really relate well to me, anyway). If I happen to be wearing a sundress made in a light-weight, airy fabric, or a femininely styled suit, I wouldn't wear a man's watch—if I felt I might be needing to know the time, I would slip one in my bag.

115

Scarves are Great...But How Do You Tie the Darn Thing?

Scarves are so fun but they seem to be a mystery for many women—they buy them but rarely wear them.

Coordinating them with your outfit is half the battle; tying them in ways that flatter you and your outfit is the other half.

A scarf should always incorporate the colors of your ensemble. If you are wearing a green dress, for example, with a multicolored scarf, the scarf must have visible green in it—the **exact** shade of green. A tiny amount of the color in a pattern may not be able to be seen from a few paces away—check it in your trusted mirror.

And while you're looking in the mirror, check to make sure that you are not appearing to be "engulfed" by your scarf. This can happen when you tie it in such a way that it covers most of your top.

An often-made mistake is letting a long scarf hang way down on your body. This really shortens your leg line and can create a dowdy look no matter how elegant the scarf or your ensemble. In most instances, it's best if the bottom of your scarf doesn't fall below your waist line.

The pattern size of your scarves is critical to your looking great! Those of you with delicate coloring are most enhanced by small and medium size patterns and very light-weight, airy looking, larger patterns that have a light background.

I need to separate those of you that have stronger coloring. If you are one of the Contrast Color Types, you'll look great in medium and large patterns and very high contrast smaller patterns. If you are one of the Muted Color Types, you'll be most flattered by medium size patterns, large *blended* looking patterns and gutsy smaller patterns.

Larger scarves can look pretty worn over one shoulder unless you are "fussing" with them all day long. Some fabrics are more slippery than others so you may want to secure your scarf from underneath with a safety pin. It used to be that scarves were worrisome around machinery but that was more in the day, long ago, when copying machines had handles you had to turn.

One of my favorite ways to wear my charcoal-gray pinstripe suit, with its curvy jacket (the stripes are cream, as is the lace camisole I wear with it), is with a very long embroidered cream-on-cream fringed scarf over one shoulder. To shorten it, and add even more *style*, I've tied a knot in the scarf about 8" above the fringe. It drops to just above my knees in the front and back. Accessories are large pearl earrings (I have strong coloring), a strand of pearls, sheer bone stockings, gray suede heels trimmed with black suede, and a black suede bag.

If you have a Color 1 Associate near you, ask her to give a *Smart Scarf Tying* class for you and your friends and coworkers. To order a super specific, easy-to-follow scarf tying booklet, check the Resource Center.

116

Looking Beautiful When It's Blustery Outside

When it's cold outside, many women don a warm scarf—sometimes without thought of the color combination they are creating with their coat, let alone their own coloring. All of the same color principles that apply to your most flattering clothing colors and color combinations are applicable here. "Cheery" bright red scarves don't look that way on Color Types that are best in toned-down colors—any bright color can make these Color Types look overly pale, anemic, and like they had better get in out of the cold and into bed!

If you live in a climate that calls for a warm scarf at the neck nearly every day for two or three months, consider treating yourself to one or two that are really exceptional—your scarf, after all, is part of your first and last impression!

A *Sexy* Woman Can Look as Sexy in Her Glasses as She Does Without Them

Notice that I said, "can". To me, sexy is a *good* thing; I consider the word a synonym for alluring and appealing. Sleazy and dowdy are *bad* things. I want your glasses to be perfect for you and this is one of the times I wish I could see you in person!

Here are some *Smart Tips* that will help you take control of what you look like in glasses:

- Frames that follow the shape of your eyebrows are often more flattering than those that don't.

- Many of the smaller glasses are great looking, some are "interesting" looking and others look "far-out" but you need to make sure that **YOU** look great and interesting (or far-out if you like)—not just your glasses.

- **Very** small glasses that have small lenses that barely cover your eyes can possibly make your eyes look closer together and even sometimes give you a cross-eyed look. Be aware!

- **Very** large glasses are not classic, nor are **very** small glasses. Each can give you an eccentric, trendy, funky, and sometimes "interesting" look.

- If you choose to wear frames that are more "substantial" (thicker frames versus a fine metallic frame, for example) it's best if the frame follows and covers your eyebrows, so that you won't have a double eyebrow look.

- Avoid glasses that "droop" down on the cheek, angling toward your jaw line—they can create a "down-line" that can make you look tired and old—*yikes!*

- Please avoid glasses that have fancy detailing across the bridge of the nose; they definitely draw attention to the nose area and can make your eyes look closer together as well as make your nose look big or "strangely" shaped.

- Embellished or "fashiony-looking" glasses can limit your use of earrings and necklaces—if you wish to wear glasses that make a definite statement of their own, keep your earrings and necklaces very simple, or don't wear them.

- If your glasses are like those described just above, and if you can afford a second pair, you may want to invest in a simple, but elegant, pair that you can wear on days when you wish to make a *different* statement.

- *Please* avoid lenses that are tinted rosy, yellowish, amber, bluish, greenish, or any other color that gives your skin a bruised look or "strange" coloration under and around the eye.

118

Framing the "Eyes" of the Soul...

Smart frames:

- Metallics and "frameless" looks are more versatile than colors.

- If your skin tone is golden, or your hair has golden highlights, your best metallic will be gold.

- Silver frames can work well with ivory and pink skin tones and platinum, ash blond, ash brown, silver (gray), or white hair colors.

- If you look best in toned-down colors, select soft-tone metallics instead of those that are bright and shiny.

- If you look best in bright colors, select a brighter metallic, avoiding those that look tarnished or dull.

- For those of you who would like a "frameless" look but need more support for your lenses, consider those frames that have a minimum amount of metal.

- A typical plastic frame does not usually look elegant enough for all of your day and evening looks.

Tortoise shell frames appear more casual than metallics and frameless looks. Your most flattering tortoise tones will be a combination of your skin tone and hair colors. They may be fine for daytime attire **if** you are *always* wearing colors and color combinations that work well with this two-tone look—usually your beige, camel, brown, cream, and perhaps, black.

However, tortoise or any tone-on-tone frame, is not dressy enough to be worn out to special dinners, cocktail parties, or black tie affairs. So if you are to only have one pair of glasses, avoid the limitations of tortoise, tone-on-tone casual looks, and colors. Unless you are an eccentric dresser, frames in colors need to be worn only when your outfit is (or has in it) the same color.

119

Getting the Best Support from Our Underlovelies

What we don't want others to see

- Bulges that show above and below your bra and your panties.
- A slip that shows in your kick pleat when you walk.

- Your bosom appearing to be an "odd" shape.
- A visible panty line.
- Seams in bra cups—own seamless bras in neutrals and colors you need.
- You pulling your panties down in the back when you don't think anyone is looking.
- Bra straps, no matter what the fashion magazines show.
- A light bra under a dark top or a dark bra under a light top.

120

Why is Shopping for the "Perfect" Bra Such a PAIN?

Unfortunately, unless you are buying the identical style from the same manufacturer you must always try them on. All 34Bs are not made equal and that's actually good—if they were all the same, few of us would ever find a good fit!

One 34B woman may be fuller at the bottom of her bosom and less full on the top; the next may have a wide space between her breasts but her breasts may go all the way to her underarms; and yet another woman may have literally no space between her breasts and they may not go very far toward her underarm (she's "all out-front"). Viva la difference!

An alluring *shape* depends on the PERFECT FIT. There are women in the underlovelies departments that have been trained to fit you in a bra—ask. A bra that fits you well:

- Gives you a great shape from the side and the front—always take the time to put your top back on (or drape it over your front) in the dressing room when you are trying on new bras.
- Does not ride up in the back.

- ◆ "Tacks" (touches) in the front between your breasts.

- ◆ Fits you well in the cup (both in the top and bottom of the cup).

- ◆ Gives you support from underneath your bosom so that you could actually slip the straps off your shoulders and "they" wouldn't fall.

- ◆ Does not dig into your skin anywhere.

121

They Ride-Up, They Ride-Down and They Can Cause "VPL"—Perhaps the Problem in Finding Panties That Fit Just Right, Like a Bra, Has to Do With the Fact that Our *Derrieres* Are All Shaped Differently!

For the best fit, most women need to buy their panties a size or two larger than they usually do (also, some panties shrink when washed and/or dried in a drier). Try panties on (over your own) in the store. Sit down. Stand up. If they ride-up or down, don't buy them. If they make a "**visible panty line**" (VPL), they are too tight or they have been cut too small around the leg opening. Own both beautiful briefs and bikinis.

By the way, bikinis and bathing suit bottoms should be worn with the sides pulled up slightly, giving you the longest and most beautiful leg line—most important when being viewed in them by your lover.

Briefs (buy sexy styles with high cut legs) are sometimes handy to tuck your top into when you need an extra smooth line. Tucking colored and printed tops into skin tone briefs is a great way to camouflage the top so that it doesn't show through lighter skirts and trousers.

122

"Slipping" One On

Slips may seem old fashioned to some of you, but they are a staple for women who wear knits, other stretchy fabrics, and unlined skirts and dresses. Slips help garments that would otherwise cling, glide beautifully over your body, and help knits keep their shape.

Own slips in black and beige (and white, if necessary). You'll want short slips, semi-short slips, and long slips if you wear skirts/dresses in several lengths. Buy slips that have a slit and line it up with the slit in your skirt—no slips showing in slits, please! Do you need a full-length slip? If you have a knit dress or a phobia, you may.

A "short story"...

A client, the president of a multi-million dollar company, brought over a couple of suits to try on for me. She had on a full length slip and it was 98 degrees outside and the humidity was 98%! Because her skirt was lined and she was wearing a blouse that you couldn't see through, I explained that the extra layer wasn't necessary. Missing my point, she assured me that she would never wear a "half-slip" again!

It seems that she was walking down a major avenue in one of our major cities and suddenly she felt something around her ankles. She looked down in horror to find her slip around her ankles—the elastic had given way.

I expect that all of you already know this but just in case, if your skirt is lined, it's not necessary to wear a slip. And except at work and church or synagogue, it isn't necessary to wear a slip under a dress or skirt that is supposed to be fairly transparent.

123

Getting Even *Smarter* Yet!

Always feel as good about your underclothes as you do your over-clothes. No safety pins in bra straps, no holes in panties. Remember what your mother taught you? You never know when you might be in an accident!

Wear matched sets—don't be *caught* in white panties and a black bra, for example. For the times when you are wearing dark tops and light bottoms, or vice versa, own some panties that are black with a small amount of white or beige on them and some panties that are white or beige that have a little bit of black. By the way, if you don't look great in black, you won't look sexy in black underlovelies. With your darker colors, wear navy or "surprise" colors.

Matched sets also means wearing bras and panties that *look* like they are a set, like lace bras with lace panties or with panties that have a touch of lace.

Color and style coordinating your underwear (your first layer) with your inner wear (your second layer, like a *base*); your inner wear with your overwear (your third layer like a blazer); and your overwear with your outerwear (your fourth layer, like a coat) can be a real puzzle at first, just like this paragraph! But, once you get the knack of it you will be amazed at how easy it is!

124

More Underlovely Details

- ◆ Wear "surprise" colors when you are wearing something you can't see through. A surprise color is *any* color that looks great on you that would be "unsuspected" under what you are wearing—like green or fuchsia under navy or black; a leopard print under black or red; or pink under purple.

- If you have a top that's cut wide at the shoulderline and your bra strap tends to show, sew in the little snaps with the threads attached that capture your straps and keep them invisible.

- Small, thin shoulder pads with velcro should be part of every woman's intimate apparel wardrobe—own them in black and beige (and white, if necessary).

- Nearly "total body control" is available—survey the latest at your department store. The one-piece undergarments that are made to "smooth you out" from your bosom to your lower thighs are valuable under dresses or at any time when you want/need to look and feel "smooth" to the touch. These "support" garments are really great because they give you the flexibility to wear things that you might not otherwise try.

- Avoid control garments that squeeze you "up and out" or "down and out", causing rolls, lumps, or bumps in places they're not welcome. Also, avoid those that will rub you raw.

- Keep some special lingerie designated for *play* and *passion* that is as appealing to the eye as it is to the touch—no scratchy lace, *please*.

- ALWAYS wear, every day, underlovelies that you would love to be *caught* in; although you may not be, *you'll* know! You'll even "walk" differently!! Try it and see!!!

125

Making Your Very First, and Very Last *IMPRESSION* of the Day

What's the first impression you make, to yourself, to "him", and to your children, in the morning and perhaps the last you make at night? You in your robe and slippers or you in a "nightgown"—I'm using nightgown as a synonym for a sleep shirt, T-shirt, tap pants and a camisole, and pj's. And if you sleep in the nude, I'm talking about whatever it is that you slip on in the morning when you get out of bed. Here are some *Smart Tips* for "naughty and nice" first and last impressions:

- Have everything in great colors and your most enhancing clarity!

- Wear a robe in an elegant length—one that covers your ankle bone or one that's short (as short as short-shorts, just covering your derriere, is a super length because it gives you the longest leg line).

- Don't wear anything that has become dingy looking.

- Wear slippers that coordinate or match—a good basic style looks like a ballet slipper with a low-cut vamp.

- Of course we need our *warm* slippers, too. Husbands might understand, but wearing slippers that look like rabbits, bears, dogs, or Mickey around a possible Mr. Right is probably not a good idea. Until a fellow gets to know you, it can be difficult for him to make the leap between "spicy lover" and cartoon slippers.

- Pajama bottoms should be a flattering length—one that covers your ankle bone.

- Washable silk pj's are fantastic, pretty, and sensual, yet "modest" enough to wear around children, house guests, and unexpected company!

- Wearing just the top of pj's, especially when it's his, is as sexy as wearing one of his dress shirts (perhaps the one he took off the night before).

- Definitely have a few "things" for private parties of two!

126

The Perfect Wrap

Are you making a negative "arrival and departure" statement? Your coat needs to make a good impression because it is often your first impression, your last impression, and sometimes your only impression.

When you take your coat off, are people surprised at what you are wearing underneath? Select coats in styles and colors that go with your clothing styles and colors. Great colors are your most used neutrals, your hair color, and core colors.

The more *basic* the coat, the more versatile and the more things you can wear it over. If you want versatile coats, make certain that:

- Your coat is long enough to cover your longest skirt—I think that coats that come just about to your ankle are very elegant.

- You have an outerwear jacket that covers the length of all of your suit jackets and blazers.

- All of your coats and jackets fit with ease over your suit jackets and blazers.

- The coat or jacket has matching buttons so as not to interfere with your accessories.

- The coat or jacket is free of contrasting or sporty stitching, epaulets, and tabs.

- It is made out of a fabric that looks dressy enough to wear day and night, over a suit to work and over a beautiful little "perfect" dress out to dinner and the theater in the evening.

- You choose the style carefully. If you tend to dress more feminine elegant, do not purchase a coat that is trendy looking, or is severely tailored, for example.

- If you love long, fuller skirts, take this into account when you buy a long coat, because if it is too straight it will be difficult for you to walk without feeling "stuffed".

- If you belt your coat, *please* make sure that you don't look like a sausage—an hour-glass, fine; a sausage, no! Belting styles with large or obvious pockets below the belt add to the concern.

- If your belt ends up making your bosom look "low", belt the coat more loosely and *angle* the knot down as you would a belt buckle.

- If you tend to wear your coat open a lot, single-breasted styles are often more flattering than double-breasted styles.

You get the picture—make sure that everyone looking at you gets a pretty one, too.

127

The 3 Coat Capsule

Have you ever had to change your mind about what you wanted to wear to a party or a special event because the weather changed and you didn't have the appropriate "wrap" to wear over it? If you answered "Yes!", or if you are tired of an overstuffed closet filled with coats and outerwear jackets that never seem to look great with your clothes, this capsule will set you free!

Coat 1

This "rain" coat follows the guidelines above, in that it is perfectly plain with no sporty or contrasting stitching, no tabs, and no epaulets. The buttons match, and it's long enough to cover your longest skirt or dress. It will look as good over a suit as it does over a "special" little dress, jeans, or anything between—in other words, it will take you from car pooling and work to cocktails.

Fabric

Your fabric is dressier rather than sporty and choices include: silk, rayon (and the sueded versions of these), velvet, smooth dressy looking cottons, micro fibers, suede, ultra suede, light-weight wool gabardine, and some leathers.

Color

A solid color, because patterns aren't as versatile. Your choices include your hair color or your most used neutral. Could it ever be a core color? If one of your core colors is your "signature color" and if it goes well over most all of the other colors in your wardrobe, yes.

COAT 2

You may not need coat 2 if you live in a moderate climate where you don't need anything warmer than coat 1 (or coat 1 with a warm zip out lining).

If you do need it, this is what it looks like: It is just like coat 1 but warmer! It can be a totally different style but the details, or lack thereof, are identical. This coat needs to keep you warm on your coldest days.

Fabric

As warm as necessary. Will furry looks work? Maybe, but not if you ever need a really warm coat in the early fall or in the spring when (by the conventional way of thinking) it's too early or too late to wear fur.

Color

The choices are the same as Coat 1.

COAT 3

This coat has a special purpose: it covers anything coats 1 or 2 don't. What would that be? Black tie, formal event attire. Don't go to any? Then you don't really need this jacket, but you may want it anyway—if you choose "just right", this jacket will be as great looking with jeans as it is with evening clothes.

What does it look like? The sleeves need to be big enough around to fit over the sleeves of an evening dress or beaded jacket (for those of you who don't attend dressy events, think big enough in the sleeve to wear over a bulky knit sweater or blazer). It's long enough to cover any evening jacket (picture a beaded jacket, for instance) you may wear, so usually mid-hip to fingertip length. It's as plain and free of detailing as coats 1 and 2 and if the neckline is high (with or without a collar) it will "cover" any neckline your evening attire might have.

Fabric

Silk, satin, velvet, dressy rayons, and some micro fibers or other "dressy" fabrics that you feel would work nicely over *any* evening attire. What about fur? Of course, "as long as" it's not sporty looking in any way (no leather inserts, leather trim, or sporty buttons); AND you'll only be needing an evening jacket when it's *cold* outside. It depends on your lifestyle and your climate—you may want both a fur jacket and one in fabric, or perhaps you could get by with just the fur and a beautiful shawl. Furs in your hair and hair highlight colors will be exceptionally stunning on you.

I love wearing my velvet "evening" jacket and my fox jacket with my jeans—it's sort of an elegant, funky look!

Color

Black (only it you look great in it), cream/off-white or other best neutrals. Consider "champagne", your best beige or camel, especially if your hair is light to medium in tone. Women with red hair should consider "copper" shades an option.

128

Adding "Variety"

Of course, most of you are going to own more than three coats—you probably already have three times more than that! The point is, in all of those coats and jackets that you do own, most of you don't have what you *need*—appropriate wraps to wear over any ensemble, for any occasion. Once you have your *basics*, you can add coats, jackets, capes, and shawls to your heart's content!

One extra that I have found so very useful is a wool and cashmere shawl that is wide enough to cover my suit jackets and plenty long enough to wrap around me—because of its length, it almost looks like a cape. I use it mostly on those fall and spring days when the temperature in the morning starts in the mid-'50s and by afternoon, it's in the '60s. I also use it on colder days when I know that all I'm going to be doing is running from the house to the car and from the car into someplace warm.

Also useful, warm, huge squares (4' to 5') that you fold corner to corner that you can wrap up in, or when it's not so cold, simply drape over one shoulder. They don't have to, but mine have a 2" fringe all the way around—I have one in black, one in navy and one in cream.

Last year was the first year that I needed a navy wrap; I didn't have any navy in my wardrobe until I found the most stunning jacket for 75% off the outlet price! Instead of investing in a navy coat or outerwear jacket, I decided I wanted to duplicate my huge warm square scarf/shawl so I went to the fabric store and bought a piece of thick navy wool and cashmere fabric—I fringed it and yes, although it is very simple to do, it takes a while. You'll want to ask someone in the fabric store how to fringe the "corners".

A "classic" trench style is too casual to be coat 1 or coat 2 (unless you are **always** dressed casually), which just happens to make it perfect for a possible addition to your capsule. Trench (and wrap styles in general) look particularly smashing when they are mid-knee or just above, or very, very long, all the way down to your ankle. It's important to check the length *with* the belt tied or buckled.

Avoid wearing below the knee length or mid-calf length coats over wider leg trousers. Also, wearing an outerwear jacket that is shorter than your sweater, jacket/blazer, or top is for certain funky, eccentric looks only.

Avoid coats that have a "half" belt in the back that scoops down, because beside the fact that they make no sense at all, they can make your derriere look droopy and/or wide! The same goes for belts on trench coats and raincoats that end up being tied or buckled in the back. The only exceptions are those that are tied or buckled HIGH ENOUGH so that they don't drape down over your "bum".

129

Hats—Topping Off Your Look with Style

Hats can be so romantic, so dramatic, and so fun but it seems that women love to buy them but rarely have the *nerve* to wear them (perhaps they just need some *magic dust*, you'll find out). Let's bring them back in style! How? Simply by wearing them.

It used to be that a woman without her hat and gloves was not appropriately dressed and I know we don't want to go back to that strict edict any more than we want our hemlines dictated. But if more hats are seen "everywhere", more women will feel comfortable wearing them, and before you know it, they'll be back. Will you be the first of your friends to start the trend? Maybe they won't follow your lead, but if you love hats, they could end up being one of your "*signature statements*".

Hat styles, of course, need to compliment the shape of your face (and work with your hair style), and without seeing each of you in varying styles, it's hard to give advice. One thing I can say is that if your face is long or an oval that tends to look long, avoid hats with high crowns and small brims (these styles are great for women with round faces and broad faces). Reach instead for a hat with a low crown and wide brim.

Since you are training your eye, go to a hat department or hat store and try them on—don't forget to check yourself from the side. Oh, another thing. If we are going to bring back hats, a veil, for certain occasions, is very romantic and exotic. Yes, I'd like to keep romance alive!

130

Elegant Hands

Socks and gloves have two things in common. Both keep our extremities warm and both often end up with one of the pair missing! I rarely make it through a winter without losing one, or both, of my gloves. I think that the lockers at my gym swipe them while I'm working out; drugstore checkout counters steal them; and I think my car snitches them from my lap because when I get out of it and get in the house; I don't have them anymore!

If you're like me, watch for sales and buy them in either your coat and jacket colors or your shoe and boot colors. Gloves that are a little longer (at least 2" or 3" above your wrist bone) are a better investment than shorter gloves because they can be used with both sporty and dressier coats and jackets. Also, you don't get a cold gap (or an inelegant gap) between your glove and your sleeve when you reach for something—like the steering wheel.

Leather and suede gloves, unless they have sporty stitching or casual detailing, are dressier than those made of wool and acrylic—especially those that look like you could wear them to shovel snow.

On my first day in Vietnam, I headed straight to the market and I noticed a large amount of very long (at least to mid-upper arm) gloves for sale. They looked just like evening gloves that you might wear with a strapless gown. They made me *wonder* but I was so busy with other "wonderments" that I forgot them until I noticed that most all of the women on bicycles and motor bikes were wearing them and it was hot outside! Guess what? It's their form of sun-block—the gloves are used to keep the sun off. They also wear baseball caps and scarves, tied like masks, over their faces.

If hats "come back" in a big way, will we carry or wear "dress" gloves with our suits and dresses, like we did in the '60s and before?

131

Singing in the Rain

Buy an umbrella large enough to keep the rain off you, and perhaps another—the smaller size is handy to carry and fine when it's just "raining" but not at all useful when it comes to a "rainstorm". Because most umbrellas are reasonably priced, make sure you always have one that is in good repair, because if it isn't, you won't be making a good first impression.

As far as color goes, most of you are probably thinking "basic black" but if black isn't great in a large amount on you, take a look at your coats and outwear jackets to see what color will match, or coordinate with, the majority. Solid colors, of course, give you the most versatility.

132

Setting the Boundaries Between Day and Evening

Because women started wearing "embellished" clothing in the daytime, metallic shoes and belts for both casual and dressy, "statement" belts anytime and "wearable art", the boundaries between day and evening wear have been totally blurred. But we do get to break all of the old rules, right? Yes, with two exceptions: **"Always Look Great!"** and **"Dress *Smart*, Act *Smart*, Be *Smart!*"**

With few exceptions, most women appropriately attired for their workplace will avoid:

- Sheer, see-through fabrics;
- Showing cleavage;
- *Very, very* short skirts;
- Anything that is too bare;
- Anything too tight; and
- Garments or fabrics that are too glitzy or very evening looking.

133

Crossovers

Velvet and silk can be used for day and evening, as can satin when it's in the form of a blouse, a camisole, or tank worn under a jacket. Warm weather allows all kinds of silk outfits in the daytime and the evening. Cold weather puts the same silk ensemble into the "evening only" category. Sueded silk can look less dressy than the smooth and shiny silks. Satin brocade trousers could be worn with a more "subtle" but stylish jacket by those of you who can dress arty, ethnic, funky or more trendy at work—they are "after-hours" pants for everyone else.

Animal prints are great for everybody, day and evening, but restraint is advised when it comes to considering *how much*. Where you work depends on whether you can wear just a touch (like collar and cuff), or bit more (like an animal print skirt paired with a solid color jacket).

A single animal print accessory, like a bag, shoe or belt, can be a fun touch with otherwise solid color attire. What about two "touches" like a belt and shoes or skirt and cuffs? I'll say yes, hesitantly. The hesitancy comes from knowing that some of you will then take license to wear three "touches" at the same time and maybe even add animal print earrings. *Please, please* don't—it's easy to step over the line here and turn animal attraction into fashion victim!

134

Being Overdressed or Underdressed

One of the things that happens when you look "pulled-together" and stylish is that you appear more *dressed-up* even in your jeans. One of my associates mentioned that she and her husband were out to dinner with another couple, and although the other woman was equally as dressed-up, she appeared to be more casual. Why? Because she was wearing toned-down colors when her best clarity was clear, bright, and bold.

My advice is that you just get used to the fact that when you look great every day, people will notice and some will comment! It doesn't mean that you are overdressed.

Never wanting you to look less than your best, I still want you to be aware that there are times when you will want to be thoughtful about what you are going to wear to specific occasions.

Have you ever had to fight the urge to go all out when you wanted to look dynamite? Why fight it? Because you don't want to "upstage" your hostess or the guest of honor. A few months ago I was faced with this situation.

A "short story"...

I was invited to the home of friends to a black-tie, seated dinner for 20 on a Wednesday night—the day of the week is significant because weekday black tie dinners are sometimes viewed as less formal than those held Friday or Saturday night. My "thoughtfulness" about what to wear came from the fact that the guest of honor was a queen—also attending, a prince and princess. Throw into this mix the fact that the hostess, always stylish and chic, usually dresses in an understated manner.

Another factor has to be added to this equation. My position as one of the founders of the image industry and an international trainer of image and style consultants dictates that I always have a certain aura—just like you in your given field, I need to look and act like I know what I'm doing.

What did I wear? I decided on a beautifully cut long black velvet dress that has a high neck and long sleeves. Sound boring? Not this dress! It has a fairly sheer black panel on the top that shows a hint of cleavage and another sheer panel in the skirt that shows a bit of leg.

My stockings were a sheer tint of black (otherwise you wouldn't see them through the sheer black panel); black shoes, of course; and my accessories were one ring, simple black and crystal earrings, and *magic dust* (you'll find out). Because I make such a statement just in this dress alone, I would have definitely felt overdressed in more (or glitzier) jewelry.

Please note that I said that "I" make a statement in this dress, not that "the dress" makes a statement! You want to look fantastic head-to-toe, not just your ensemble. How did I come across? Well, I must have lived up to my profession because the queen, a really beautiful, elegant, stylish, and incredibly nice woman, asked for copies of my last two books—*How to Be Sexy Without Looking Sleazy* and *110 Mistakes Working Women Make and How to Avoid Them: Dressing Smart in the '90s.* I will be sending her a copy of this book, as well.

135
What About Being "Underdressed"?

Since you are *now* in the habit of dressing appropriately for the occasion, when you find yourself in a situation where you appear underdressed, I'll assume that it really was an accident. Sometimes we just get swept-up into what's going on—we're invited to "stay-on" or go out with friends who have forgotten to mention that the last part of the day, which started out casual, involved a black tie affair. When this happens, your poise, self-confidence, and elegant attitude will get you through. Anyone there who would think or say something unkind is not self-confident, nor are they elegant. Part of being elegant is never making someone else feel inelegant, "small" or *less*.

What if you are invited someplace and you don't know what the expected dress is? Try to find out—it's very *thoughtful* of the person doing the inviting to inform his/her guest what the attire is, so that's the first person I would ask (and if he didn't know, I would ask him to find out—also, be sure to ask him what he is wearing). Mothers, *please* teach your sons that when they ask a woman out, she finds it so thoughtful when he gives her an idea about what to wear, or even just tells her what *he* will be wearing.

It's difficult to make a good decision based on insufficient data, but if it's impossible to find out the expected attire, consider the factors that you do know (time of day/evening and expected length of stay, weather and place of function). Then, paying attention to these factors, get ready to create a special memory, regardless! What would I do if I knew nothing? Put on a *base* with some nice, but not "glitzy", accessories and add a simple, but very stylish jacket— no problem, I've got my *magic dust!*

136

The Romance of Evening Attire

Do you buy evening clothes that fit your Princess Di fantasies or your real-life lifestyle?

I love my overly romantic nature as much as some of you love yours—after all, if we don't "fight" to keep romance alive, what will become of the world? But sometimes even romantics have to be practical.

If you only attend one dressy event each year, this section of your closet should occupy less space than it does in the closet of a woman who attends a black tie function once a month. Want to attend more events, celebrations and "parties"? Create them! Make them happen!! What are you waiting for—you can always find a reason to celebrate, honor, rejoice, or frolic!!!

If you do dress up quite often, creating *bases* for evening will help keep you sane. Wearing a different jacket (velvet, beaded, satin, embroidered) over the "same old" base can create a totally different, yet bewitching, look.

For a holiday party at work, wear a green or red velvet jacket over a cream-colored base. For New Year's Eve wear a beaded jacket over the same base and for a wedding, wear an embroidered jacket. For certain events, you could even forget a jacket and add an incredible belt and/or a beautiful shawl.

Depending on the fabrics of your bases, you can dress them down by wearing them with a suit jacket. For example, a wool crepe base in one of your favorite neutrals or core colors can go almost anywhere, depending on your jacket and accessories.

Shop for evening clothes before you need them. There is no more harried shopping experience than one where you have to find an ensemble for a special occasion RIGHT NOW! If you have an evening base in your closet, and you find yourself in this unsettling position, all you have to do is look for a new jacket.

In your evening dresses (and in any top), *please* be aware that if the side of your bosom is visible, or your neckline is cut so low and wide that you can see the crease **under** your breasts, no matter how firm you may be, these "angles" make your bosom look as if it is sagging! With sleeveless and strapless dresses, be aware of the potential of skin *pooching-out/up* near your underarms. A change of bras might fix the concern.

Bias cut dresses are "magic", and very alluring, on **every** size and shape woman. Even if you are a plus-size, don't hesitate to try on a *small*, (yes, I mean that the size in the neck says "small"). Just hold out the fabric and eyeball the dress's true potential of fit. So, don't forget to check all sizes when you are shopping for a long dress.

Sleeveless, strapless, and otherwise bare evening dresses most often need skin tone/nude stockings and, probably, **never** semi-opaque or opaque stockings.

Please don't just add crystal or rhinestone earrings and/or necklace and think that they are appropriate with your evening attire. You will want to take into account all of your *Smart Tips,* making certain that your jewelry is making the same statement, from both a color and style standpoint, as your costume. Clear, bright crystals and rhinestones are not super on Gentle or Muted Color Types because they "pop" off the body, making your eye go straight to the bright spots instead of to the face.

137

Cinderella's "Magic" Glass Slippers...

Own shoes and evening bags that match your base exactly. Add metallic, and other most used evening neutrals, when/if you feel they will be important in "finishing" a specific *costume.*

Please avoid wearing flats with evening dresses unless you are a young teenager—and they probably won't even want to!

Your balance is thrown off by wearing light metallic shoes with darker evening wear. What seems to be happening is that the fabrics of some evening dresses have a metallic "fleck" in them that women are matching for their shoes and bag. Your full length mirror will tell you if there is enough of this metallic fleck, seen from a distance, to create good balance with a matching metallic shoe. If it's "iffy", don't do it.

Similarly, you can't just wear silver or gold metallic shoes and matching metallic earrings with any dark dress. No, not even if you carry a matching bag. No, not even if you add a matching necklace—"light" shoes with dark clothing do not create good balance.

Many evening shoes, even those that are not sandals, have "fancy" straps or detailing. If your ensemble has a touch of compatible detailing, fine; but if your "costume" makes quite a statement on its own with its styling, design, or because it is embellished, a very simple, low-cut (in the vamp and on the sides) shoe with a slim heel will make a much more elegant statement. By the way, few evening dresses look good with a shoe that is the least bit clunky-looking or has a thick heel.

138

Makeup Can Be Magic or Tragic

If you have a plastic bag or shoe box filled with makeup you've bought (or think you got free) that you've barely touched, raise your hand.

Repeat after me:

"Makeup is fun, but ruining my budget isn't. I promise to make every purchase count toward making ME as gorgeous as can be."

Pick which makeup trends to follow as carefully as you would a fashion or a fad! If the "experts" in the fashion and beauty magazines told you that the only way you can look stylish this year is to wear all of your skirts 5" below or above your knee, 95% of you wouldn't listen. You would go on wearing all of your most becoming skirt lengths! The same *NEEDS* to be true about makeup, but it isn't.

For the past few years, while brownish lip colors have been the trend, I've spent lots of time shaking my head. Muted and Gentle Color Types (and Cross Color Types that look best in toned-down colors) have looked pretty good in some of the least brownish of them. Meanwhile, Light-Bright and Contrast Color Types (and Cross Color Types who are more flattered by clear colors) have looked *really* bad in them! Drab and dull!! **WE WEAR MAKEUP SO WE WON'T LOOK DRAB AND DULL!!!**

One of the oddest things about this particular lip color craze is that most women never wear brown clothing and if you ask them why they'll tell you it's because they don't look good in brown. Yet they've been wearing it on their mouth, thinking they look great!

ALWAYS create a makeup look for yourself that compliments your coloring, using your best shades in your best clarity. No matter what is "in" fashion, stay true to your coloring if you want to look young, fresh and vibrant.

139
Wearing the "In" Looks

Each of you can do *your* best version of a makeup trend, it's just that if you don't know your "best" makeup looks, it is going to be difficult to figure out your best version of a trend.

A "short story"…
One of my beautiful black associates who looks great in clear, vibrant colors wanted to find her best version of a brownish lipstick. Because she is aware

of how fabulous she looks in clear colors, she could judge each brownish lipstick against that radiance. Having to reject them all, but being a very creative woman, she found that she could get her best version of this look by combining just a hint of a slightly brownish lipstick with one of her clear, bright lipsticks.

Experiment, but know what looks phenomenal on you so you'll have something to judge against—remember, the new look should be "**equal to, or better than, the best look you have right now**"!

We are beginning to see more and more bright colors in lipsticks on the shelves and in magazine ads. The makeup companies want to sell you something "new" and everybody already has enough "browns"! Now I have the opposite "worry". Women who are most flattered by toned-down clarities are beginning to wear the "new" brights and they are looking pretty bad—overpowered, garish, overdone! But, those women who look great in clear colors and are wearing the "new" brights are looking fabulous! You get to decide whether to follow a trend or pass it by.

140

In Need of an "UPDATE"?

Wearing your makeup just like you did in high school or college almost always makes you look *older* and *dated*. If you just got out of school you will probably want to develop a stylish look, perhaps one that is more "polished', that compliments your new work image. And if you've been out of school *forever*, you may need to give yourself a reality check to make sure you're ready to begin the new millennium with style!

The "look" that you wore in high school or college may have worked for your face and your image at that time (maybe not). But just as styles change over time, so do our faces, and because we look at them every day, we may not notice subtle changes that may greatly benefit from a different way of applying our makeup.

Every few years, spend some time "playing" with an expert who will show you how to keep your look contemporary. Take what you learn and "interpret" that new knowledge into a makeup style that will work for you—keep in mind your most flattering clarity, colors and color combinations.

141

Looking "Finished"

Some work places don't "require" a face full of makeup but no matter where you work, you will always want to look great. For most of us, that means wearing at least some makeup.

How do you know how much you need? Aim for a "finished", head-to-toe look. That means if you are wearing a suit, or its equivalent, your face needs to be equally as "dressed". If you are wearing the latest trends to work, you'll be making the same statement with your makeup. A sporty-casual look certainly doesn't *require* eye shadow but you can still wear it—although there are no hard and fast rules here, a little lighter application is usually a good statement match. A visual alarm goes off when your face doesn't make the same statement as your outfit—it's like, "What's wrong with this picture?"

What's your "bare" minimum look? Mine is the finest line of eyeliner, mascara (but not always taking the time to use an eyelash curler), a hint of blush (just what's left over on my brush from the day before is fine), and lipstick. This takes just two minutes and I feel so great about the way I look that I could open the door and be delighted to find a favorite former lover or my "first" husband with his wife (I've only had one husband, by choice of course, but I love referring to him as my first). Speaking of first husbands...

A "short story"...

After a Color 1 Associates training in Tokyo, I flew on to Hong Kong with my co-trainer to do a little shopping (the trip and some shopping money were a bonus for her). We got in late and I told her that the next morning I was going to dress very casually and just do my "minimum makeup look"— we had been "dressed to the nines" for 11 days of training and there was no way that I was going to do more! Besides, we were going to be going to the famous Stanley Market and it was really hot and humid outside.

Well, wouldn't you know! The next morning we're in the coffee shop about to order breakfast when I look up to see my first husband with three other men—all of them dressed in suits and ties! I *immediately* got up and went over to give him a kiss (yes, he's a really exceptional man). I smiled at the other men and said, "It's good for William's reputation to be kissed by strange women in coffee shops."

How did I feel about the way I looked? Fabulous! That's why I didn't hesitate for a second in going over to him. When you don't feel good about the way you look, the tendency is to hide from, or avoid, not just first husbands but life and lust. What was I wearing? "Magic Dust" (you'll find out), black cotton shorts, black leather sandals with rubber soles, a black T-shirt with a silver metallic eagle on it, a black and silver belt and a black baseball cap. My "minimum makeup look" of lipstick, a touch of blush, a fine line of eyeliner, and mascara made the perfect matching statement to my outfit.

How little makeup can you get away with and still feel great about the way you look? Make a decision and do it for *yourself* every day. Yes, even (especially) on the weekends!

142

Developing Necessary Skills

Women are not born with the skills to apply their makeup artistically so they can end up looking overdone or underdone. Find a person who can help you learn to apply flattering colors of makeup in differing ways to fit all the parts of your lifestyle. If you know your best look for work, how do you vary that look for casual evenings and dressier evenings?

Don't trust everyone wielding a makeup brush to show you your best looks—sometimes makeup artists just teach the "latest" look (read: trend) and most are trying to sell makeup—it's their job. Hoping to sell you more, they use lots of products on you (they are trained to do so) when only a few are necessary to achieve a great look. Ask for a "classic" makeup lesson. Once you know the *Smart Basics* (free advice available at www.dressingsmart.com) for your face you can learn some trendy "tricks" to use from time to time, depending on your lifestyle.

Women's magazines and makeup books have some good information and some misinformation. It can be difficult to correctly relate their advice to your particular eye shape and face shape but you will probably always learn something worthwhile. The advice in magazines is most often trendy so be aware that these makeup looks may not be your best and/or appropriate at your place of business. Also, they may be "out" just about the time you master the technique.

143

Practice Makes Perfect but Perfecting the Wrong "Placement" or Technique For Your Eyes and Face is No Help at All!

+ Is your eye shadow placement or your eyeliner making your eyes look smaller instead of larger? (I didn't wear eyeshadow until I was 35-years-old because every time I tried, even working with a "professional", my eyes looked *smaller*.)

- Is your eye makeup moving your eyes closer together instead of wider apart?

- Is your blush placement making you look older?

- Are the lip and blush colors you are using making you look vibrant, "hard", or drab?

144

The *Universally* Most Common Makeup Mistakes

- Foundation too dark, too pink, or peachy.

- Using concealer incorrectly.

- Too much makeup.

- Too little makeup.

- Too brownish or orangy blush.

- Wearing a lipstick and blush together that do not compliment each other.

- Wearing too brownish a lipstick for your coloring.

- Wearing lipstick that is too bright for your coloring.

- Not matching your lipstick and blush to the red, plum, fuchsia, raspberry, or coral clothing you are wearing.

- Too reddish eyebrow pencil.

- Over-plucked/too thin eyebrows.

- Not "sketching" in missing eyebrows at outer edge.

- Too much, too dark, eyebrow pencil.

- Not brushing your eyebrows "up".

- ◆ Putting blush on forehead, nose, or chin.
- ◆ Wearing too much blush.
- ◆ Wearing blush in the wrong place.
- ◆ Too brownish lip liner.
- ◆ Using unflattering eye shadow colors and not getting the placement right for your eye shape.
- ◆ Too much eyeliner.
- ◆ Using eyeliner in such a way that makes your eyes look closer together or smaller.
- ◆ Not blending eye shadow enough.
- ◆ Not removing dark visible hair from upper lip and chin.

145

Getting *Smarter* About Foundation

Your foundation must match the skin on your neck **exactly** in natural daylight—you don't *wear* it there, you only match it there. Don't let anyone talk you into "warming-up" your skin tone or "canceling" out undertones. With your makeup on, you should be able to stand naked in natural daylight (*Yikes!*) in front of a mirror and have the color of your face match that of your body.

It's difficult to find the perfect foundation but getting it right is worth **immense** effort! One reason it is so hard is that most makeup lines do **not** have enough (if any) golden beiges, slightly golden ivories, golden camels, golden browns, ivory beiges, or light ivories (that aren't too pink) to choose from. If you need your perfect foundation, check the Resource Center.

146

Concealer, *Itself*, Shouldn't Show

It's supposed to help hide our red spots and our brown spots but "**it**", also, should not show. Choose a concealer that matches your skin tone as closely as possible—mix it with some of your foundation if necessary. This mix also gives you a consistency that is easier to work with.

Placement of concealer is very important and almost always done **incorrectly**—*please* do not cover the entire area under your eye. If you put concealer on a puffy or swollen area, the "puff" will look bigger, not smaller—and definitely not concealed!

Usually, what you're trying to conceal are dark circles under your eyes and other "rotten" spots. The dark circles are usually found just *under* a puffy area. Using a tiny brush, the tip of a small sponge applicator or the tip of a cotton swab that is well-formed (not a fluffy bigheaded one) apply a small amount on the darkened area **only**. "Pat" it carefully to blend—avoid rubbing it as it can end up being spread onto areas where you don't want it.

There's a lot of discussion about whether concealer should be used under, or on top of, foundation. Whichever works best for you is fine with me, however many women don't need concealer once they've skillfully applied the **right** shade of base. If you apply concealer first there is a tendency to rub it off, or move it out of place, as you are applying your foundation.

147

Wearing *Too Much!*

One of the most aging looks in the world is too much makeup, especially too much foundation and powder. How much is too much? Too much *looks* thick and if you ran your fingernails gently down your face and got foundation under them you are definitely too heavy handed! Keep your goal in mind—you are after the look of a beautiful *even* complexion, not layers of product.

Sometimes an overly made-up look comes from wearing too bright, or dark, lip and blush colors, not too much product. Double check your best clarity and also know if your coloring is delicate or strong looking. **On delicate coloring, less looks like more!**

I think I'd ask a perfect stranger whom I felt looked very "together" if she thought I was wearing too much makeup—you can take a poll. Sometimes when you ask women you know, they have built-in perceptions of you (or their own agenda) and you don't get good or accurate advice. If you ask a makeup artist in a store, she generally has **not** been trained to know what's best for YOUR coloring.

148
Wearing *Too Little!*

You may also ask a stylish stranger (again, probably not a makeup artist) if she feels you are wearing too little makeup. If you most often feel like you look washed-out you probably need more makeup of different colors (perhaps brighter, clearer colors) and/or to change your clothing colors. Check your best clarity and note that **on strong coloring, less makeup looks like even less!**

149
The Radiant Glow of a "True" Blush Color

Wearing a blush that is brownish or orangy is the fastest way to take away your radiance. You just don't blush orange! All women are very flattered by their body's natural red color—you'll see this color in your finger tips, your palms, and your unmade up lips—it is the color you blush naturally. Other becoming blush colors are your best plum or fuchsia, raspberry, and red-coral (that's your body's natural red with just a touch of pinky-coral mixed in). **Avoid brownish blushes no matter what the shade, unless you want to look older!**

150

Getting Coordinated

One of the things that I thought every woman already knew about makeup, but obviously doesn't, was that her lipstick and blush should be the same color, or very, very close in shade. Exceptions are made for trendy, funky, eccentric and arty dressers.

Lipstick and blush also need to be the same clarity—your best. So, if you are wearing a clear, bright fuchsia lipstick, your blush will also be a "clear" fuchsia. The exception to this *Smart Tip* is the blush you wear with coral and pinky-orange lipsticks. Since many coral, and all orangy, blushes can sallow, gray, or muddy your skin, it is important not to wear a blush that is any more coral or orange looking than one that is just a hint more coral than your best shade of red. Think of this color as falling right between your best red and your best coral.

151

The Fastest Way to Looking "DRAB" or "FAB"

Just like brownish blush, wearing too brownish a lipstick can instantly take away your healthy glow. As in all other fads and fashions, they aren't for everyone and you get to decide if a new trend works for you. Would you wear stockings with seams or padded skirts every day, just because they were all the rage? Twelve-inch skirts? Bejeweled glasses with "wings"? Blond hair with 1" or 2" of dark roots showing? Grunge? The drugged-up look of "heroin chic"?

Those of you who are most enhanced by clear, vibrant colors need to avoid all brownish lipsticks. For those of you who look radiant in more subdued, toned-down colors, choose your brownish lip colors carefully. If they look like mud, or gray or dull the skin around your mouth, you'll know you need a lipstick that has, at least, a little more *color* in it.

152
"HOT" Lips

Wearing lipstick that is too bright for your coloring can make you look all mouth—so that's where "his" eyes go when he looks at your face.

Sometimes guys stare at your lips just because they find them sexy, not because the lip color is too bright. For years I had a *major* crush on a man who always ended up lowering his eyes to my lips when we were talking. Your best clothing clarity is absolutely the clue to your best lipstick and blush clarity!

153
Yet Another Way to "Get it Together"!

I really thought every woman knew that if she was wearing a raspberry or red dress or jacket, for example, that her lipstick and blush should match that exact color. Obviously, since I've been shaking my head about this for several years now, this fundamental explanation has not been passed down from mother to child. Again, exceptions are made for the trendy, funky, eccentric, and arty dresser.

When a woman wears a brownish coral lipstick and blush, for instance, with a red or raspberry suit she looks as if her head and her body belong to two different women. This is one of the reasons that so many women today do **not** look well pulled-together although they may be trying their best to look great.

It's very simple; all you have to do is have a "makeup wardrobe" and a clothing wardrobe that both go with YOU! If you do, you will automatically own a lipstick and blush that will coordinate beautifully with all of your clothing. Besides matching reds to reds, plums to plums, and so on, here are some examples of lip and blush colors that are wonderful with some of your other best colors—there are no "hard and fast" rules here, just some of my favorites. You can develop your own:

- ◆ Wear any of your best lip and blush colors with white, off-white, cream, beige, camel, brown, gray, navy, and black.
- ◆ Try your best plum, fuchsia, or raspberry, with greens, blue-greens, robin's egg blue, and teal.
- ◆ Wear any of your best shades with blue and purple.
- ◆ Try your best plum, fuchsia, and raspberry with red-purples.
- ◆ Wear any of your best shades with yellow.
- ◆ Try your best plum, fuchsia, raspberry, and coral with rust.

154

Framing Your Eyes

Your eyebrow pencil needs to match your eyebrows exactly or be just a hint lighter or darker. Many "supposedly" brown eyebrow pencils are too reddish and only work well for women with reddish hair. And some of the pencils for "blondes" *write* so ashy that they can instantly drab a woman's glow.

Some women need to use two different colors of pencil to get *their* eyebrow color just perfect—it's worth the effort! For example, if a "taupe" pencil is too light and a brown pencil is too dark, simply combine them. When it comes to which to put first, try both ways on the back of your hand—use your eyebrow brush to blend the colors together. If a black pencil seems too dark and the brown is definitely too light, you now know what to do. For **fabulous** shades of brown and "blond" eyebrow pencils and brow definers, check the Resource Center.

155

Yikes! Please Don't Take Too Many!

Thin-line eyebrows were a fad that some women continue to follow. Watch over-plucking your brows because eventually they may stop growing back and you'll wish you had more. Also avoid "drawing on" eyebrows more than just a hair line above, or below, your natural brow line. And *please* don't shave them off and draw them back on—yes, some women do.

156

Connecting the "Dots"...

One place where most women, after a certain age, need to add two or three hairs is at the outer edge of the eyebrow. These missing hairs can make your eyes look closer together—sketch them in and watch your eyes appear to be further apart. Your eyebrows are like frames for your eyes and if the frame stops short, they look unfinished.

How far out should they be? Hold a pencil at an angle from the bottom corner of your nose to the far outside corner of your eye. The extension of the pencil will show you a good stopping place for your brows.

157

Too Much, or Too Dark, Eyebrow Pencil Can Make You Look Older (*yikes*), or Hard!

Lighten up your touch, or the color you are using if necessary, and keep your pencil sharp. Blend with an eyebrow brush. If you are using a brow defining powder, apply it lightly just where you need it. I find this "powder" perfect to cover/coat my "silver" eyebrow hairs—I have three or four.

158

Taming the "Wild Ones"!

Many women run around with their eyebrows in "disarray", giving them a scowl or a tired or unfriendly look—especially if they are brushed down. Always brush them up (and slightly over, if necessary)—it's like getting a free eye-lift! Try it both ways and you'll see what I mean.

159

Placing Blush in the Right "Place"—the Look of Whisker *Burn* is Not Cool

Red or rosy chins can make you look like you have whisker burn. A red nose can make you look like you have a bad cold, you've been out in the cold or you've had a bit too much to drink. Why would anyone want to create any of these looks on purpose? That's what you are doing if you put blush in these places. Foreheads don't blush either! Brush these old myths right out of your mind!

Blush is used to create a natural glow and is best kept to your cheek area. These guidelines will work for every one of you, whatever your face shape—this "universal" *Smart Lesson* is actually very **unique** to you:

- Do not place blush any closer to your nose than the inside of the iris of your eye.

- Do not place blush close to any part of your eye—keep the "eye socket" area and smile lines (or other lines) free of blush.

- Do not place blush any lower than the bottom of your nose.

- Do not place blush as high as your temples.

- If you want to make your face look wider, place your blush nearly horizontal.

- If you want to make your face look less broad or less round, place your blush at a slight upward angle.

If you follow these guidelines, you will find the exact placement for *your* face. Remembering to always apply powder to your cheeks (in a downward motion) before you apply your blush helps it go on much more smoothly.

There are two other things that need to be mentioned here. First, *please* don't put the **TIP** of your blush brush in your blush. A blush brush was meant to apply blush by stroking first the blush and then the face with the long hairs. If you have a small space to work with, turn the brush on its side.

Try stroking your blush and your face going with the long hairs and see how much easier it is to apply and blend. *Please* don't approach either your blush, or your face, with the bristles of your blush brush pointing toward them. If you do, the bristles of the brush go right into your pores, filling them with blush, making it nearly impossible to blend well.

As you approach your face with your brush, avoid starting to apply your blush at any edge of the parameters of your placement. Start instead in the center of the area you want your blush to cover, and then blend out, over and down. If you start by placing your brush at the bottom of your nose (your lowest parameter), once you've "blended" your blush, it will end up lower than your nose. The same thing happens if you start at the inside of the iris of your eye, by the time you've blended the blush, it will be too close to your nose. Practicing the *perfect placement* does make perfect!

160

Two-Tone Lips—Do You Look Stunning or "Gruesome"?

Two-tone lips can be very beautiful but they can also look really bad if you line with a lip liner that is too brownish for your coloring. For a classic makeup look, the lip pencil should match your lipstick as closely as possible. For a beautiful "fashiony" two-tone look, keep the colors and clarity fairly close to each other and at least very close to **your** best.

161

Keeping It On...

One day after having lunch with two of my beautiful and stylish friends, they announced that they had been purposely watching me eat to see how I managed to keep my lipstick on throughout an entire meal—they'd been wondering (whispering, I'm sure) about this for years! It's easy, and I thought everybody already knew this tip but it's in this book just in case you don't.

Simply color your entire lips with your lip pencil and then put lipstick on top. A lip pencil "stains" your lips so that when you eat-off your lipstick you still have color on your mouth. Also, I "blot" my lips gently with my napkin instead of wiping. So now you all know!

One day I even made it from 7:30 a.m. to 5:30 p.m. without needing a touch up. My day? I flew to Cleveland (from Washington) where I made a presentation to the president of a company, then had lunch with the chairman, and made it all the way home—I'd actually forgotten my lipstick; thankfully I didn't need it.

162

A Few *Smart Tips* for Your Eyes

I wish I could give you some good solid information on how to apply eye shadows but without seeing each of you individually, it's impossible to do a good job of it. These "universal" tips will help:

- Avoid using colors that make your eyes look bruised.

- Place light colors in small spaces that you want to look larger—for many women, that means keeping your eyelid area light.

- Place darker colors in spaces that you want to recede.

- Place shadow in such a way that your eyes look more wide-spaced—lighter colors, or lighter application, on the inside (toward your nose), and medium or darker colors, or darker/heavier application on the outside. Of course, if your eyes are "wide-set" you don't have to create this "illusion" unless you want them to look even wider apart.

- Those of you with strong coloring can wear more eye makeup without looking overdone than those of you with delicate coloring— each of you can have a dramatic look when you like, it's just that if your coloring is delicate, it takes less to create the drama!

163

Blend, Blend, and Then Blend Some More!

Blend your eye shadow unless you are going for a fashion look that calls for something different. For *classic* eye makeup, you shouldn't be able to discern where the shadow stops and starts. After you've blended *really* well, blend it again.

164

How Much Is Too Much When it Comes to Eyeliner?

It depends on the time of day (think a.m. makeup and p.m. makeup), where you are going, and what you want people to think about you when you get there.

What's your goal? For your eyes to be more notice-able, not your eyeliner! If eyeliner is all you see when you glance at your face, it's too much (which can mean too heavy or too dark). Smudge it. Look again. Narrow the line. Look again. Soften it by using a cotton swab to take some it off. Look again. When you get it right, the focus is on your eyes, not the liner.

If you want your eyes to look further apart, don't line all the way into the inner corners. If your eye lids are hooded, or show very little space above your upper lashes when you look straight on (versus looking down or up) at yourself in the mirror, skip dark liner on your upper lids or make the line very, very fine. If you don't, your eyes will look smaller, not larger, and more closed, instead of more open. Fine lines need a pencil with a very sharp point. If you need a **great** pencil sharpener that gives you the sharpest point without quickly "eating" up your pencil, check the Resource Center.

165

"Contouring" Your Face Is Best Kept for Photography!

You aren't fooling anyone into believing that your nose is shorter or narrower, or that you have hollows below your cheeks. You just look like you have smudges on your face or that you were too heavy handed with your makeup.

166

Remove All Unwanted Hair from Your Face as Often as It Takes to Keep It Perfect!

No exceptions.

167
"Creating" Beautiful Skin

If you have beautiful skin, I hope you know how blessed you are. It's so difficult to do a good job of applying your makeup if your skin isn't in good condition. I don't care whose products you are using, if they aren't working for you, you need to change them. If you are feeling loyal, perhaps the brand you like has different formulas that you can try.

One of the most important things is finding someone who will work with you to get your skin lovely—someone who will give you samples to try *before* selling you a bottle or jar of something that may not work.

Did you know that the greatest cause of breakouts is *over-moisturizing?* In this "day and age" of fear of *aging,* the first thing a woman does is reach for a moisturizer. She thinks, the richer, the better! If you are breaking out, this may very well be the cause. Check it out!

168
Crowning Glory or
Serial Bad Hair Days

Too many women get "all dressed up" to go to work and their hair ruins their image. If you are having a "bad hair day" it can ruin your day, as well. Take any measures necessary to get, and keep, a hair style that works **for** you, not against you. Some *Smart Tips:*

- Dirty or uncombed hair is not appropriate in any business situation—wind-blown, messy on-purpose looks are different than uncombed hair. How? One looks un-cared for, the other should look pretty and natural.

- If you are wearing your hair like you did when you were in high school or college, the style is more than likely no longer as enhancing and contemporary-looking as it could be.

- Hair that has no movement (sprayed until frozen) is not *smart*.

- Find a stylist who will keep your look *smart*.

- Always check the back of your head for "hair holes"—I believe that's a southern term. The back of you is as important as the front, because if someone sees the back of you first, he may never be interested in seeing the front.

- A great hair cut is only as good as you can make it look on a daily basis—get one that you can manage.

- Find someone who can cut well—*consistently*. A good hair cut may cost as little as $15—a good hair style may (but not necessarily) cost more, but once it's styled you can have it *maintained* by anyone who cuts well. It's best to show it to the person that will be maintaining it (you're showing him/her a new "pattern") within the first week or two of when it was styled.

169

Stay Away from the "Brassy" and the "Ashy"!

There's just an awful lot of hair out there that is too ashy or too brassy looking. If your hair is brassy looking, it can sallow your skin and/or give you an inexpensive appearance. If it is too ash, it can gray and dull your skin, taking away your vibrance and causing you to look washed-out.

Your hair color is critical to your image and if the color is wrong it can really diminish your beauty, even if everything else is perfect. Find a good colorist—not necessarily the same person that cuts or styles your hair.

170

Damaged Hair, Damaged Image

If your hair looks damaged, it damages your appearance! Get the damaged part cut off and then vow to keep your hair in good condition.

171

No Obvious Roots of a Different Color—No Exceptions!

If you are not going to keep your color or highlighting up, *please* don't color or highlight in the first place!

172

Matching "Statements", Again

Hair styles are particularly effective when they look great on you *and* with what you wear on a daily basis—your hair and your attire need to make the same statement.

Trendy hair is great if you get to dress that way at work—otherwise, it may be "undoing" your career goals. And this goes for "big" hair, extreme asymmetric cuts, matronly looks, and highly dramatic and old fashioned styles (unless you're into drama or retro). Hair ornaments (bows, clips, and combs) should be understated when used with *classic* clothing and more "serious" looking business attire.

Change your hair stylist if you don't constantly get a look you love—"loyalty" can keep you looking out of date or just plain frumpy!

173

From the Tips of Your Fingers to the Tips of Your Toes, Polish Creates *Polish*

Color on your toes? For me it's a must because I feel very naked and totally unsexy without it. My "much" older sister recently told me that when she was 5-years-old she remembers meeting our Aunt Anne for the first time. She was mesmerized—it was the first time she'd ever seen polish on toes and she thought that our aunt was the most glamorous woman she had ever seen.

No dirty nails, ripped cuticles, or chipped polish at any place of business, ever. If keeping your polish in good repair is a problem, use a clear finish, only.

174

Wear Colors AND Clarities of Polish that Look Great on You!

Please make sure that your polish colors are neither too bright nor too toned-down because if they are, the skin on your hands can look gray or muddy—that translates to *OLD*. If you like the white tip "French" or "American" manicure, make sure that the tip isn't too white for your coloring. Also, if you wear a lot of cream instead of white, a creamy-white tip will look great!

For *classic* attire and most places of business, make sure that the color you have selected matches (fairly closely) your lipstick and/or goes with your attire. Unless you are a trendy, funky, eccentric, or arty dresser, no red polish with a coral, orange, raspberry, plum, or fuchsia outfit, for example, unless you are combining two of these colors on purpose.

Earlier I mentioned that one of my favorite ensembles is a fuchsia suit worn with a red-coral shell and a beautiful silk red, orange, and fuchsia scarf. With this look I often wear fuchsia lipstick and red polish.

As I write this, the continuing fad/trend for polish is in very non-classic colors like purple, blue, green, black, yellow, or green. Selling mostly to teens, but enough to adults that I need to mention it here, these colors should only go to work in trendy, funky, fashiony, arty, and eccentric atmospheres.

175

Long Nails—Alluring or "Cheap"?

Sorry, I used that *cheap* word again. I guess that I must really want you to get the "point"!

There is a point at which long nails are too long and can instantly cheapen your look. Can I give you a measurement? Yes, but some of you aren't going to like the numbers. One-quarter of an inch beyond the tip of your finger is long enough (and perhaps too long if you want a classic elegant look or have small hands). One-half of an inch is definitely too long.

I know that fashion is supposed to be fun but having jewels and art decorating your nails is a fad or fashion that only goes with some far-out trendy, funky, eccentric, or arty looks. If you are "wearing" embellished nails in the "wrong setting" you could very well be thought of as less elegant.

> *A "short story"…*
> One of my associates was judging a model search. There was a very attractive young woman who had everything going for her except that her nails were very long and decorated. They gave her a less than "classy" look and she wasn't chosen. Now, one would think that she could be selected anyway and someone would just tell her what "not to do" to her nails. But, the judges couldn't get past the *overall* first impression.

A model is a *sales* woman. She is selling what she's wearing, what she's holding, and what she's pointing to. All of the top models portray a certain elegance. People automatically admire and project positive qualities and values onto an individual whose image is elegant and stylish even though these traits may not actually exist.

We all make an instant impression and based on the way we *look* judgements are made about our character, values, wealth, importance, intellect, and personality! Once imprinted in one's mind, these impressions are hard to change. Just remember, a **positive** impression is *equally* as powerful as one that is negative!

176

Squared-Off Nails Look Like Little Shovels—Definitely Not a *Smart* Look

The first time I heard that description, I think it was in the late '70s or early '80s. The square shape seemed to come into prominence with the popularity of acrylic nails. A nail that is rounded, more oval in shape, is much more beautiful for **everybody's** hands. The square shape makes your fingernails look fake, your fingers look masculine instead of feminine, and your hands look "sturdy/stocky".

One of my friends told her husband that she wanted to go back to having acrylic nails and he fought her on the idea. When pinned down, he said that they didn't look real and that he would like it if her nails looked like mine. Well, after a short "fit", she told him that I do have an acrylic coat on my nails.

So she went back to acrylic nails. We were having tea when she showed them to me—they were square. A discussion followed that one of the reasons my nails look "natural" is their oval shape and I mentioned that "little shovels" are neither flattering nor real looking—that caused her to have another short fit.

Once she got used to the idea and the new shape, she loved it—she told one of her friends about the "little shovels" and her friend had a fit. Pass it on!

A friend of a friend (who won't tell her that her nails are sending a negative image) is a public relations executive in a large firm—she wonders why her Japanese male boss doesn't respect her. If you know her, pass it on!

177

Drawstrings Around the Bottom of a Jacket or a Top Should Be Avoided!

None of us are flattered by the "blousing" fabric effect a drawstring creates, regardless of whether it's at the waist, anywhere in the hip area, or below the hip! Perhaps you can remove the string with happy results! No, don't even wear it loosely tied!

178

If You Love Menswear Looks, Consider Wearing Them in a Very *Womanly* Way!

- ◆ A lace vest or lace shirt with all else tailored.
- ◆ All tailored but a very curvy jacket.
- ◆ All tailored but with a short pegged skirt or a longer slit skirt.
- ◆ A twin-set and pearls with pleated flannel trousers or pinstripe trousers.
- ◆ Wear feminine accessories like a lace pocket square and pumps with at least a mid-heel height.
- ◆ If you are wearing extra feminine looking makeup, you can wear your hair in any style, including slicked back.

179

Too Much Dazzle in the Daytime?

Buttons that have crystals, rhinestones, or sequins are not appropriate for most business attire. If the buttons on your jacket or dress are keeping you from wearing it to work, you could change them. Otherwise, enjoy the jacket in your off-hours.

180

Show Cleavage Only During Your Free Time

Coffee breaks and your lunch hour don't count! With your blouse buttons, when in doubt, button another.

181

Be Smart About Your Fragrance

Please avoid wearing more than a hint of fragrance to work—strong perfume is neither business-like nor sexy. A person should be able to discern another's fragrance only when in very close proximity. Use your fragrance sparingly and ask an honest friend or coworker if he can tell when you've entered the room.

Be ultra sensitive about coworkers who may be allergic to any amount of fragrance. If you work with someone like this, *please* refrain from wearing any at all.

A small closed-in space (like a car) can magnify the intensity, so when you get in the car with your "date" and he immediately opens the windows you may guess that you've been a little heavy handed with your perfume.

182

Too "Matchy-Pooh"

Too many matching details can turn an otherwise fantastic look into a "didn't know when to stop" look. For example, silver detailing and silver buttons on a jacket, silver bracelet, silver earrings, and a bag with silver studs. Trade the bag for one without any metallic details or for one with a simple silver clasp.

183

Are You "Saving-Up" for a Special Day?

If you are someone who "saves" your new or favorite clothes to wear for a special day or night, and you find that at the end of a season you have yet to wear them, you may have just missed some special times. Stop putting-off looking great—if you feel special about the way you look every day, you'll find that every day is a special day!

184

Encouraging Strangers to
Examine Your Bosom, *Yikes!*

At least not at a business function, *please!* If you are handed a name tag, if at all possible, place it just below your right collarbone. If you place it lower on your chest, it forces people to stare at your bosom while trying to read your name.

185

Don't Be Afraid to Be
"Caught" in Your Pajamas!

Just make sure that you look and feel like a "million dollars" in them. Silk and beautiful cotton pj's are inexpensive when they're on sale and you'll feel so glamorous in them that you would happily open the front door to a surprise party!

My very spicy, best friend, Phyl (a woman of a certain age), has even taken to entertaining in her silk pj's. She "hangs-out" in them and puts them on the minute she gets home from work. If friends call and want to stop by, she doesn't bother to jump back into her clothes—why should she? She already looks like a "million dollars"!

186

Creating Elegance Where None Existed Before

Make an extraordinary impression by always carrying and using a *real* handkerchief. Ask your grandmothers, great aunts and your mom for any extras they may have—they'll most likely be delighted to share. Yes, those with lace and tatting on the edge are what you are after, but more tailored handkerchiefs are also beautiful! You can find some super ones at garage and estate sales, but if you must, buy some that are new.

187

Writing an *Excellent* Statement

Please, no cheap looking pens from other companies, banks, and free giveaways. A beautiful pen makes a nice statement about you and may cost under $10. If you can't spend the money on one right now, use pens that are plain black, navy, or gray. When you acquire or are gifted with a stylish pen, you'll want to keep track of it, because just like socks and gloves, they tend to disappear.

188

It's Not *Smart* to "Chew"!

Unless you are alone and not on the phone. It looks unprofessional and inelegant. Also, it can be distracting and a major irritant to others—especially if you are "popping" it!

189

Building from Zero or Paring Down?

For those of you who desire great style but are on a really tight budget (or simply prefer a minimal wardrobe), here are some *Smart Tips*:

- If you could picture yourself wearing just one color day after day, what color would it be? Build your entire wardrobe around this color—it will become your "*signature color*".

- Buy only *basics* and *classics*—uncomplicated, but beautiful.

- Wear *bases*.

- Review the *Smart Capsule Wardrobe Tip #62*.

- Make a choice between gold and silver jewelry.

- One belt should work with everything and it should be the same color as your shoes—the buckle will be either gold or silver, depending on your jewelry decision. Remember that you can remove belt loops, removing the necessity of a belt.

- Your shoe and bag color should be the same—that color should be able to be used with all of your outfits; depending on your "signature color", consider your hair color or another color perfect neutral.

- You may need both flats and heels; make sure that they are both cut low in the vamp and fairly low on the sides.

- Review the *Smart Coat Capsule, Tip #127*, and choose wisely.

- In your "makeup wardrobe", have just one of everything you really need.

190

Traveling with Style

How proud do you feel about telling your seat mate on a plane or train what you do when asked the inevitable question? Could he guess what you do by the way you are dressed? Would she guess executive, mid-level, entry-level, or unemployed? Art gallery or boutique owner? Fashion journalist or lawyer?

What impression are you giving others about yourself and your company when you travel? Would they want to do business with you or your firm based on the way you look? Yes, you do reflect on your company's reputation, as well as your own, every time you get dressed, whether you are going around the world or just to the post office.

Travel stylishly and comfortably (remember, comfort and sloppy are not synonyms). Select your travel attire according to your arrival activities and pretend that your seat mate may be the prince you've been waiting for (forever), the president of your company, or the chairman of the major corporation you've been dying to work for.

If you are headed straight for a meeting, or are being met by a business associate, dress for business (unless you are traveling overseas, in which case you may want to travel more casually—read: elegant casual—and change into your business attire before you arrive).

191

Leaving and Arriving in Style

Although it would be nice, your luggage does not have to be the same brand, or same style. But it should be the same color. Buy the best luggage you can afford and stop using any luggage that looks like it won't make it through another trip—in other words, be proud to claim your luggage, not embarrassed.

The color of your luggage is important. Select from your best neutrals and your hair color. Avoid patterns that are not likely to compliment your traveling wardrobe and be aware that some patterned luggage looks inexpensive.

192

A "Love-Hate" Relationship
with Packing

We may love to go places but most of us sure don't want to pack! Many women have told me that before they became "clients" they used to hate to pack—it was such a major chore because they really didn't have anything they liked well enough to take. Also, it was tough because everything that went in the suitcase called for a different bag and different pair of shoes.

Since learning these *Smart Tips*, they tell me they still hate to pack! Now, their reason is that they *love* everything they own so much that they want to take it all with them! Although one or two pairs of shoes work with everything, they still want to take more—I'm just like them! Can you imagine loving *everything* you own, so much? Soon!

What to pack, of course, always depends on where you're going and what you're going to do when you get there. If I'm going to be gone more than two days I always take at least one base and usually wear another. That way, all I have to do is change jackets and accessories. If you are traveling for more than a couple of days, don't forget your *Smart Capsule Wardrobe* and remember to pack more tops than bottoms.

There are many good ways to fill a suitcase; I slip a cleaner's plastic bag over each garment that could wrinkle. I made it all the way to Jakarta with linen and silk and didn't need an iron. Packing for this trip was easy—I just needed to take 12 different great looks for 12 *consecutive* days of work.

The purpose of my trip? To train new Color 1 Associates to become International Image and Style Consultants and to present a three-hour wardrobe seminar to three hundred women, including ambassadors' wives, Indonesian fashion designers, and the press. My back-to-back schedule? Six-days of Associate Training, followed by our three-day Advanced Women's Wardrobe Training and two-day Men's Wardrobe Training, followed by the seminar.

How could it possibly be easy to find, let alone pack, 12 great ensembles? I didn't buy anything new; everything I have is a "million dollar" look and it was such a joy to pack it, knowing how perfectly everything would work once I got there. When you know you look great, you can forget about the way you look and get on with *life!*

193

Please Let Every Young Woman Experiment with Style and Color

Although I want very much for every young woman to learn, and use, the *Smart Tips* in this book, I want, even more, for them to have the freedom to experiment with fashion, fads, styles, and colors.

Yes, learning good habits and good skills is very important for them; and yes, if they follow these tips they will definitely look better—a lot better! Encouragement is good, but this isn't the time to dictate "adult" taste if it is at the expense of *quashing* their creativity.

The place to speak up, and to be firm, is if the young woman is hurting her image/reputation by dressing in a very inappropriate or sleazy manner. *Please* remember that what's inappropriate for school or work may be just fine for an outside of school or work "activity".

194

Keep Your "Million Dollar Looks" in Great Shape

Wearing a garment or accessory that needs to be repaired ruins your look—*please* don't do it! Train yourself to immediately repair, or have repaired, anything that needs it. Keep an eye out for loose threads—trim them right away because they can make even an expensive garment look less impressive.

Fix the heels on your shoes *before* they need it and shine them *before* they look like they need a shine.

Please do not dry clean your clothes to death—it really does kill them. Pressing adds more damage. Take dry cleaner plastic off clothes the minute you get them home and hang them on "proper" hangers.

If you have even the tiniest possibility of being "hit" with moths, take precautions—**do not use** cedar chests, cedar lined closets, cedar balls, or cedar blocks to protect your clothing. They do not **kill** moths. Only use moth "blocks" or balls that say right on the package that they kill moths. It's fine to use a cedar chest or cedar closet **if** you add this protection. When it's time to wear these clothing items again, you can air them out by hanging them on the shower rod for a day or two (air needs to circulate around them), or you can put them in the dryer on "fluff" with some fabric softener sheets.

If you keep any wool items in your closet during the summer months, please take the time to shake them out and brush them every two or three weeks—this should disturb any eggs that have been laid. But the best protection is total isolation with a product that **kills** moths. Clothes that have been dry cleaned are **still** susceptible to moths.

195

Bad Advice is Rampant!

I wish that I could tell you otherwise, but fashion editors and stylists continue to give awful advice and continue to show looks that won't work on anyone! I know that this sounds unkind but I am being so strong with you here because, until you train your eye and get some *magic dust,* you are **susceptible** to their words and pictures.

Here are some examples of **BAD ADVICE**, all from the most popular national magazines:

- ◆ "Petite women look best in sleek, structured designs." Simply not true! First of all, sleek, structured designs do not add even 1/4" of height to anyone. Secondly, having less height does not limit you in any way—it's all a matter of how you combine different styles.

- ◆ "If you are bottom-heavy, wear ankle-length skirts only." *Yikes,* nearly a whole country/ world of women in really long skirts! You can wear any skirt length you want; it's all in the shape of the skirt and what you pair it with.

- ◆ "Don't wear light-colored pants." Of course you can wear pants in any color that's great on you—it's all in the color combinations you choose and your skill in bringing the bottom color "up" to give you great balance.

- ◆ "Petites should always wear short skirts." So untrue! You can wear any length you want, it's all a matter of what you wear with it.

- ◆ An article on how to minimize a large bust suggests wearing a high V-neck sweater. It's true that a sweater like this doesn't call attention to your bosom but it does **nothing** to minimize it. No mention was made of the fabric—if this, or any, sweater was ribbed, tight, or clingy, it would *emphasize*, not minimize, **any** bosom.

◆ The same article said, "The boxy shape of a sleeveless turtleneck will camouflage a big bust." Actually, most sleeveless turtlenecks accentuate any size bosom but what was most alarming here was that the accompanying picture showed a clingy, curvy, not boxy shape!

◆ From an article on suits, "Big hips are best in long jackets with a high closure." Yikes! High closures have nothing to do with making hips look smaller, firmer, or nicer in any way. Now, if they read this, all women with hips larger than they wish (which are most women) may feel that they can't look great in other jacket styles! **All** women can wear all jacket styles, looking great in them simply depends on how they fit and what style bottom you pair them with!

◆ Also about suits, "Narrow waists look best with a one-button closure." What strange advice! Since narrow waists look great with all styles, why would women want to limit themselves? Actually, curvy jackets with one button at the waist are very flattering to all women!

◆ From the same article, "Shiny or bare skin shows better in a sleek suit." Picture me shaking my head! I'm not sure what they had in mind when they wrote this copy, but whichever way you take it, it's absurd.

◆ When asked what the best kind of jewelry to wear with a high-necked sweater, the reader was told to wear dangle earrings instead of a necklace but if she really wanted to wear one, a long pendant that falls below her bust would be the best. If we aren't talking classic business attire, the dangle advice is okay (unless you have a long face) but the reader was led to believe that this is the only good choice for earrings (simply not true). She is also led to believe that the choice of earrings is much better than the choice of a necklace. A variety of necklace styles work well with high-neck sweaters—in this instance I can't accurately advise because there was no accompanying picture and high-neck might mean anything from a jewel neckline to a turtleneck.

Although this bad advice came from just a few articles, you can open any major women's magazine, any month, and find inaccurate advice! How can you tell if the advice is accurate or inaccurate? You have three ways. Absorb and practice all of your *Dressing Smart Tips,* use your mirror, and train your eye.

196

Closet Surgery

Is this elective minor surgery or major mandatory surgery?

It depends on you and your closet but if you desire a brand new *you*, you may need to operate on, amputate and transplant things in your closet. Before surgery, get a good mental picture of the woman you want to be, what she looks like and your lifestyle. Steady your hand and begin.

Step 1:   **Remove everything from your closet(s)—work in natural daylight.**

Step 2:   **Evaluate each garment and separate your clothing into three piles**

Pile 1)

Those items that are worn out, hopelessly stained, you hate, are the wrong size, are uncomfortable, just don't look good on you, and those clothing items you haven't worn in a long time.

Take a second look at all of these things. Can you figure out why you hate something? Is there anything about it that you could change that would make you love it? If a garment is uncomfortable or the wrong size, can it be altered or changed in some way to make it useful?

Perhaps the things that don't look good just need a shoulder pad, different accessories, or need to be combined with a different style top or bottom. Are those items you haven't been wearing out of style? Or do they just need a little tailoring, new buttons, or simply need to be paired with something new?

Store (someplace other than your closet, if possible) things you love that are within two sizes of your current size. Give away anything you feel another person could use and toss the rest, keeping only your "newly discovered" possible treasures—for the time being put them in pile two or three. Can't stand to give away or toss an old treasured item? Put it someplace where you can go and "visit" it—not in your closet.

Pile 2)

Those garments that you like but require mending, tailoring, or cleaning. Handle these "chores" as soon as possible.

Pile 3)

Clothing you feel great in; things you like but aren't great colors for you or your best clarity; and garments you would like to wear more often if only you had more things that went with them.

For those items that are not color or clarity perfect, figure out if you can "save" them by adding a color perfect accent near your face. If not, they go in your giveaway pile. Should you keep them to wear when nothing special is going on? My advice is to give them up unless it means you'll be going naked. You'll never feel good about the way you look in them and the days you wear them will definitely not be special!

"Back in the days" when I still worked with private clients, on Capital Hill there were entire Congressional offices filled with my clients (including the senators/congressmen, their wives, and staff). When a new staff member joined one of these offices, she/he were "talked-into" calling me for a consultation. The newest "convert" would tell me that when individuals came in to work in the morning, she/he would create a buzz—what someone was wearing would be a definite "b. J." or an "a. J.", before JoAnna or after JoAnna!

Now it's time to look at those garments you would love to wear more often and make a list of things you will need to purchase to accomplish this. If you want to take them shopping with you, as soon as you finish step 3 you can put them in a bag and *get going*. Do I sound determined to get you organized?

Step 3: Coordinate your outfits and take notes

First, how many *bases* can you make? If you changed contrasting buttons to matching buttons on a blouse, would it complete a base? Do you have any dresses that "look" like a base? If you'd love to make more bases, add to your shopping list the colors of tops or bottoms you'll need to accomplish this (take with you the top or bottom you're going to match).

How many jackets do you have that will work over your bases? If you changed some buttons, would you have more outfits?

How many separates can you "coordinate" into intriguing looks by bringing the bottom color "up" with a necklace or a scarf; by using a belt and shoe in the same color; or by combining like values of colors, like two pastels, for example. If you need to shop for some neck accessories that match your bottoms, add the details to your list. What about other finishing touches like earrings and necklaces, shoes and bags? If you need shoes and a bag in your hair color, they go on your list.

Remember that mental picture of the *new* you? Keeping it in mind, are there any "holes" in your closet? If most of your things are too casual to wear to the place you spend 40 hours a week, that's a big hole! Add needs and desires to your list—the needs will make your wardrobe work for you and the desires will help make your life work for you.

Step 4: Put your keepers back in "Your Favorite Boutique"

One good way to organize your "boutique" is by garment—a separate section for: suits, jackets, dresses, trousers, skirts, tops, and evening wear. Use good hangers—the investment will pay you back by keeping your clothing in good shape. I know it's not always possible, but hang as many tops as you can (including sweaters on padded hangers)—it's very easy to forget to use things that are folded and put away in a drawer.

Placing "cubes" on top of your closet shelf is a great way to keep everything else organized and in full view—and, the top of the cubes gives you a second shelf. My cubes house my sweaters, tops (that aren't hanging, including T-shirts), bags (including totes and brief case), and my collection of wild jeans—one of my "*signature statements*".

Shelves for your shoes (versus those pointy metal things) are fabulous. You'll never regret the investment—buy them at one of the super hardware stores. Count how many shoes you have before you go so you'll know how many shelves to get.

The shelves can be stacked so that you can get several shelves into a small space—try stacking them under your top, jacket and suit sections. Too many shoes? Store those that are out-of-season (elsewhere).

In my boutique, part of my belt collection—another one of my "signature statements"—hangs on tie-racks and the other part (larger belts) are placed on a small, rattan four-shelf unit that I got at an import store. To make it look even more like a work of art, I've actually draped some of the belts over the top and others around the rattan wrapped side "poles" that hold up each shelf.

All of my necklaces, those I wear and those I don't at the moment (they are treasured gifts or are works of art that I love) are hanging on a wall in my bathroom. If you think that your significant other might object to this "exhibition of art", perhaps there is a closet wall or a wall behind a door that usually stays open that you could use. It's often a hassle, and it's time consuming, to look through little boxes and bags in a drawer—if you can see your necklaces easily, you will use them more.

Earrings can be separated in any way that seems to make sense to you. Little cabinets that have lots of drawers, like apothecary chests (they are good for necklaces, too), are wonderful, as are larger jewelry boxes with small drawers. I have one drawer for my earrings that have black on them (black and gold, black and silver, black with crystal), one for my cream and white earrings, one for my silver and gold earrings, and one for earrings that are a color.

If possible, hang your scarves in your closet (or your dressing room, if you are lucky enough to have one) where you can see them. When they are tucked away in a drawer, they usually get less use and often get "messed-up" as a result of having to look through them to find the one you want. Mine hang on wooden dowels whose original purpose was to hold wine glasses upside down.

Make your closet(s) as light-filled as possible! Unfortunately, many women have to deal with peering into dark closets, trying to decipher colors, especially whether the garment is black or navy. One friend solved this problem by putting little gold safety pins in the labels of everything navy. She also put little blue dots in her navy shoes—it saves her numerous "trips" to the window or a lamp.

View your closet as you would any other room in your home, with a fondness for the way it looks and for the things that are in there! Keep everything neatly hung and find little ways to "decorate" it. I have some of my more romantic evening bags, and some sachets, hanging here and there—the way my belts and scarves are "displayed" add to the ambiance!

Buy a special notebook or journal (one that you love when you look at it) and in it write down all of the outfits/ensembles you have created—don't forget to include all of your accessories and the color of your stockings.

As you wear each of these outfits, I want you to place a little gold metallic star by those that you feel are your "million dollar looks". Place a silver star by those you feel, at least at this time, are your thousand dollar looks (*good* looks), a blue star by your hundred dollar looks (*okay* looks) and a red star by all other looks (perhaps *acceptable*, but not so special). You can buy a small package that contains all of these stars at the office supply stores.

As soon as you have time, try on each of your looks that has any star other than a gold star. See if you can figure out what you could *adjust* about this look that would turn it into a "million dollar look" or at least one that you could give a silver star.

Change the color of the stars in your notebook when you've accomplished this. See if you can move all of your red-star outfits (in this case, red means danger) at least up to a blue. If you can't, perhaps you can do without them—that doesn't mean, necessarily, that the entire outfit gets tossed because *pieces* of it may combine with other things to create a "gold star" look.

197

So You're Going Shopping, Again!

Once, when Loehmanns was a great place to find unique bargains, a friend flew into Washington to shop, bringing with her a friend who had just gotten divorced and was in need of both an "uplifting" experience and an "update" of her wardrobe—she needed *date* clothes!

After about a half-hour of collecting things for them to try on, I put them in the dressing room—for those of you who don't know, at Loehmanns everyone undresses and tries on in full view of everyone else (they've since added some private dressing rooms). I kept going in and out, bringing more things for them to try.

On one of my trips in, a woman came over and asked where I was finding the clothes I was bringing in. My friend said, "She's shopping off the same racks you are!"

One of the reasons we were causing such a stir, and why everyone was watching us, was because I was only having them try on clothing that would look great on them from a color standpoint—their best shades, clarity, and color combinations. And, of course, from a style perspective, I only brought in neat looking "stuff". The result was that they looked great in almost everything!

Some women just want to give-up and wear any old thing because they are exhausted by their lives. One of the things that leads to this exhaustion is the constant hassle of trying to deal with a wardrobe that doesn't work. Shopping with a trained eye makes all the difference! Armed with all of your *Smart Tips* I'm sure you're going to be successful and have fun, too. Here are some reminders:

♦ Visit "Your Favorite Boutique" (your closet) before you go shopping.

- Don't forget to take your list of any thing you need that will complete, accessorize, or pull together something you already have.

- Wear something you like that is easy to get in and out of.

- Wear comfortable, but good looking, shoes that are easy to slip off and on.

- If you'll be wearing stockings with most of what you're shopping for, wear them when you go shopping.

- Wear full makeup and make sure your hair looks good!

- Don't shop when you are tired or in a hurry.

- Keep focused but keep an open mind—even when you're shopping with a list, you may find something unexpected. If it's returnable, take it home to see if it fits the "you" you want to be.

- When you are attempting to change the way you look, avoid shopping with a friend who says, "That doesn't look like you" when you ask her/his opinion—it's not the old you that you are shopping for.

- Shop with a small shoulder-bag worn across your body—it gives you such freedom that once you try it you'll hate shopping any other way.

- Many of us love the look of "shabby chic" when it comes to decor—now, unless we have an endless supply of money, we need to think "inexpensive chic"—buy great looks anywhere! Forget about labels; pretend that you are in a foreign country and you don't have a clue as to the prestige level of the store. Shop for style, quality, and price! I know that some of you get your self-assurance from a "label" but when you are truly confident that you look great, the fun and pride will come from knowing that you don't need to wear designer clothes or brand names to look like a million dollars!

- Don't get hung-up on the size marked on a label, or on the size marked on the racks you are shopping from. Learn to "eyeball" a garment and you can almost always tell if it will work for you without looking at the size. When I have time, I check every size. You'll be surprised at what neat things you will find in the small and medium sizes that will fit nearly anybody and what you'll find in the larger sizes that will look *smart* on someone who is petite! If the size on the label bothers you, cut it out.

- Don't buy anything that isn't **equal to, or better than, the best look you have right now!**

- Whatever you buy, take it back to "Your Favorite Boutique", coordinate it with existing items, and try everything on. If you still don't have the look **YOU** want, return it. If you did just create a new look that will bring you "oohs and aahs", write the winning combination in your notebook of "million dollar looks", gold star it, and start wearing it immediately! Don't save it!! Don't put off getting all of those compliments!!!

Keep in mind that salespeople have their oddities and that their "advice and comments" may not be true for you (after all, they don't know who you are, or who you desire to be) and their advice may be inaccurate. I am grateful to many salespeople for their helpfulness and caring and it would be nice if they had color and wardrobe training to help clients, but few do. If the fashion magazines are offering bad advice, what can you expect from most salespeople?

Also, all color advice from salespeople is suspect—
YOU need to take control of your most flattering colors, clarity, and color combinations.

A client, shopping with her color chart, reported her experience with a salesperson who, upon seeing her chart, said, "Oh, you have one of *those*. You don't really believe in *that*, do you?" She also told me about the salesperson who ran all over a different store, only bringing her things to try that were in colors on her chart. These helpful salespeople have found that clients are much more willing to try **and buy** styles that they never would have considered, just because they are in one of her best colors. Guess which salesperson gets the continued business and referrals?

198

A Quick Reference Check List to Dressing *Smart*

An exceptional look is attained, in part, by paying attention to all of the "little" components that make up the bigger picture. Here's an abbreviated check list:

Mirror:	Full-length, use it to view your front, side, and back.
Your look:	Stylish, perfect for your career and personal goals.
Ensemble:	Perfect styling for you (line and design); beautifully coordinated, totally elegant "million dollar look" whether it's casual, businesslike, arty, classic, ethnic, eccentric, trendy, romantic, feminine, high-fashion, vintage, funky, dressy, or formal.
Color:	Great shade for you.
Clarity:	Not too bright; not too toned-down.
Color	Not too strong/overpowering;

Combination:	Not too weak/washed-out looking.
Pattern size:	Perfect for your Color Type.
Fit:	Perfectly tailored for you.
Underlovelies:	Always beautiful; a perfect fit, giving you the perfect shape.
Jackets/tops:	Paired with the perfect style bottom.
Necklines:	Compatible.
Shoulderline:	A tiny bit wider than your hipline—create a "V" shape.
Hemline:	Any of your best lengths paired with perfect jacket/top, stockings, and shoes.
Trousers:	Long enough; paired with perfect top/jacket, stockings, and shoes.
Hair:	Stylish.
Makeup:	On—neither too much nor too little.
Stockings:	Perfect color, weight, texture, and fit.
Shoes:	Perfect style, weight, color, and condition.
Earrings:	Right statement and color for your outfit; right shape for your face; right size for your Color Type and hair style; metallics match.
Necklace:	Right statement, color, and size; works with your earrings and with the shape of your jacket/top neckline; metallics match.
Bracelet:	"Quietly" perfect; same statement; metallics match.
Watch:	Color perfect band; same statement; metallics match.
Ring(s):	Compatible styles; same statement; metallics match.

Pin:	Perfect placement; right shape; same statement; metallics match.
Bag:	Perfect style, color, size, and condition; same statement; metallics match.
Belt:	Color perfect; same statement; metallics match.
Coat/jacket:	Same statement; compatible color; long enough.
Comfort level:	Good or great.
The way you feel:	"Like a million dollars"!
What you have:	Magic Dust (you're about to find out).

199

Developing a Signature Style

If you desire to be unique, to truly set yourself apart from other women, you'll want to learn to transform the same (or slightly different) clothes other women are wearing into your own distinctive "*signature statement*".

Why did I say the "same" clothes other women are wearing? Because there are only so many good styles to pick from that you are bound to be putting your *signature* on something that several other women have purchased as well—never mind, you are going to look so great and so "you" in it that it won't look the same!

What could your *signature statement* be? Anything you want it to be! Here are some ideas:

- Always wearing a beautiful scarf, tied in both simple and amazing ways.
- Always wearing a skirt with heels when other women mostly wear pants with flats.
- Always wearing the same color or variations of the same color.
- Always wearing an incredible belt.

- Always wearing the same style—all ethnic or all arty looks, for example.

There are those among you who will find this boring, but for those of you who don't, think of how easy it will be for you to develop this *signature statement* once you have decided what it will be.

Let's say you love scarves and feel that they will be a perfect *signature statement* for you. Not only will you collect scarves, but you will master the art of only buying clothing pieces (specific necklines, solid colors, *basics,* and *bases*) that work great with them.

Curious about my *signature statements?* You've been reading about them. I collect incredible belts, amazing jackets, and "wild" jeans. Because of the belts and jackets, I love *bases!* My jackets are all styles from long to short, so my favorite shape trouser is a narrower cut and my straight skirts are pegged. Because my jeans are "wild", I pair them with wonderful solid color tops and *basic,* but well cut, stylish jackets.

If you like the idea of a *"signature color"*, you have just made your life unbelievably easy and fun. You can pick a color like purple, or a neutral like cream or black (if black looks great on you head-to-toe). You could even pick two colors that you love to combine (that most others don't think to combine) like blue and green, green and turquoise, blue and turquoise, blue and purple, or fuchsia or plum with an orangy-red, coral, or a pinky orange.

You can even choose two neutrals, like cream and camel (not for those of you with strong coloring), or one color and one neutral, like red and black (not for those of you with delicate coloring)—*please* remember to keep your best color combinations in mind.

Once you've established your *signature color(s),* shopping for anything, from coats to accessories, becomes so easy! At a glance, when you walk into a store or up to a rack of clothing, you can instantly tell if there is anything you even want to look at, let alone try on. Think of how few shoes and bags you'll need. But, will you get bored? Some of you will and some of you won't. If you get bored, it's an easy remedy. Just start another *signature color* or add another *signature statement—* belts or scarves, for example.

Will you look great every day? If you are practicing your *Smart Tips* and using your most becoming shades, clarity and color combinations, you will look incredible! Will people think that you are eccentric? Maybe a few. Smile. Others won't even realize what you are doing, they'll just think that you look wonderful all the time. Most people will think you are a very attractive and *interesting* woman.

If anyone gets "verbal" with you about it, you can either share this book with them (a very gracious act) or ignore them and let them continue to muddle through, keeping their "hit and miss" habit of looking good one day and not so good the next.

200
The Unexpected Gifts of *Dressing Smart* with Great Style

When you feel great about the way you look, you *interact* differently with **EVERYONE**, and the impact of your self-assured behavior touches many lives, bringing you incredible abundance in your personal life and your career.

Your truly extraordinary *gift* to others is the positive, radiating effect you have on everyone whose life you touch and on those people whose lives they touch.

When you feel confident about the way you look, your relationship with your significant other is more "delicious" (okay, maybe just better). When things are great at home, he's different at work and that impacts on his job performance and his relationship with his coworkers. When things are great at work, the coworkers go home happier and that happily alters their relationships with the people in their lives.

Think about how your self-esteem affects your children, their happiness, the way they interact with each other, and the way they behave and succeed at school. If a child is doing better at school, think of how that adds to his/her self-confidence; think about how that self-confidence inspires his/her teacher, affecting the teacher's work—with your child and all the others—and the teacher's home life.

Your self-assurance, self-confidence, and self-esteem are making all of this happen!

Beyond doubt, the way you feel about yourself will "gift" you with the same amazing impact on your life (present and future), your work performance, your co-workers and the lives of the people they touch.

I didn't write this book to show you how to be beautiful, I wrote it to show you that you already are. My wish for you is the best gift of all, the gift to yourself of MAGIC DUST. Yes, it does exist! It is a potpourri of self-love, joy, and contentment!! Mix in a large amount of heart and soul and just the right touch of attitude, sprinkle it on yourself, and you'll have miracles and "zillions" of enchanting days and nights!!!

JoAnna

Dressing Smart in the New Millennium

228

The following resources are directly available through JoAnna and Color 1 Associates. For the latest information, or to purchase any of these resources, please visit JoAnna's Web site: www.dressingsmart.com, or call her at 202/293-9175.

❏ The Sensual Little Book of Secrets

How To Be Sexy Without Looking Sleazy: Although this little book has an amusing title, it is a gem! Based on interviews with men from all over the world, asking them what they find sexy versus sleazy, JoAnna wrote it for conservative women who wish to look more sensual without "stepping over the line". It was featured in *Cosmopolitan* (the Brazil *Cosmo*, too) as well as three other women's magazines.

❏ Personal Consultations

Color 1 Associates International Image & Style Consultants: To "change the way the world looks at you" by working with one of the most talented, experienced, and most respected color and image consulting firms in the world, visit JoAnna's Web site for information on the Associate nearest you.

❏ Color Charts

The Color 2000 Color Chart: To find out about our exciting new Color 2000 Color Charts, check JoAnna's Web site at www.dressingsmart.com— they are soooooo fun, very reasonably priced, and a super way to get your wardrobe working for you instead of against you!

❏ Career Opportunities

An Intriguing and Exciting Career—become a Color 1 Associate International Image & Style Consultant: Visit JoAnna's Web page at www.dressingsmart.com, or contact one of Color 1's exceptional Directors of Training…

- ◆ Kathleen Spike (Oregon) 503/417-1895
  email Spike@spikebizcoach.com

- ◆ Kate Frost (Colorado) 303/740-6111

- ◆ Debbie Huff (Texas) 281/578-5918
  email DSHC1@aol.com

- ◆ Maggie Quinn (Michigan) 231/947-0024
  quinnerr@email.netonecom.net

- ◆ Debbie Platzkere & Sylvia Brickman (Pennsylvania) 610/664-3198

- ◆ Lea Hamilton (Georgia) 770/304-9149
  email georgialea@aol.com

- ◆ Sachi Matsumoto (Japan) 81-45-713-2179
  e-mail Jzt05662@nifty.ne.jp

- ◆ Marianne Hauri (Europe) 41-1-932-2226
  e-mail EURCOLOR1@cs.com

- ◆ Diane Humphreys (Australia)
  61-7-5577-5869
  e-mail CreativeHorizons@bigpond.com

❑ Exotic Shopping Adventures

Go Shopping for "Treasurers" in Exotic Asia— Return with a sensational new wardrobe and an exceptional new image: Your spree will be led by a talented personal shopper from Color 1 Associates. Visit www.asiashoppingtours.com and look for Vietnam shopping tours. Why Vietnam? The prices are unbelievable and the quality of workmanship as fine as anywhere in the world!

❑ Looking Smart in the Home

Learn to be an Interior Designer the *Color 1 Way:* Or, take this extraordinary training just to learn how to put your signature statement on your own residence. Much more than just a nuts and bolts education, this hands-on experience will help you add a personal touch that most designers don't know—how to design a space and create an ambiance, that enhances the people who live there, not just the rooms of a house.

❏ Super Shoulder Pads

Super Shoulder Pads to Keep Your "Million Dollar Looks" Looking Great: These shoulder pads are for your HANGERS.

❏ Scarf Tying

Elegant Effortless Scarf Tying: Easy to understand pictures and directions make learning to tie the most stylish scarves as simple as tying your shoes.

❏ Color Perfect Foundation

Color Perfect Foundation: Absolutely necessary for having a *Smart* Image is having a foundation that matches your skin tone exactly. The colors and the quality of these products are phenomenal!

❏ Color Perfect Eyebrows

Color Perfect Eyebrows: For the most natural shades of blond and brown eyebrow pencils and the BEST pencil sharpener, visit JoAnna's Web site at www.dressingsmart.com—you'll also see wonderful brow definer colors!

❏ Television Program

Help Start a Dress *Smart*, Act *Smart*, Be *Smart* TV Program: A daily television show so that you can *experience* everything you've been reading about and *more*! The program would show *REAL WOMEN* of every size, age, lifestyle, and budget how they can be stylish in *REAL CLOTHES* that they will love and can afford.

JoAnna's audience would be made-up of *real women*, hopefully including you someday, and every segment would be run like a "workshop". She will pull women out of the audience to illustrate *Smart Tips* and all of the details you'd need to accomplish them. Audiences would be asked to wear something to the show that they would like critiqued—an outfit they need help with or an ensemble that they think is perfect but may not be.

Every show will have segments that focus on *Dress Smart, Act Smart, Be Smart.* The *Dress Smart* segment will include tips from this book and a daily makeup lesson. The *Act Smart* segment will include all kinds of wonderful "stuff" that women would like to learn more about like:

- How to be more sensual—including components from JoAnna's little book, *How To Be Sexy Without Looking Sleazy.*
- How to walk with style and grace.
- Manners for the new millennium.
- How to "sound" *Smart.*
- How and why *older* women and full-figured women can be as sensual as younger women.
- Getting in and out of cars (and SUVs) with grace.
- Attracting the type of man you would like to spend time with.
- Changing your lifestyle to make it *live up to your dreams.*
- Maintaining a sense of *mystery* and *privacy* when you live with a man and much, much more!

In other words, the show would be about clothes, makeup, and men! If you would like to help make it happen, please complete the feedback form on the following page and return it to JoAnna.

JoAnna, Tell Me More!

I'm interested in learning more. I would love to see you host a television program for women that deals with issues concerning clothes, makeup, and men. Here are some ideas on what I think should be included in such a program:

_____

_____

_____

_____

_____

_____

_____

_____

Thank you for your feedback and support.

Please return to: JoAnna Nicholson, Color 1 Associates, Inc., 2211 Washington Circle, NW, Washington, DC 20037. Fax 202/293-1060 or email JoAnna@dressingsmart.com.

Your name, address, email (optional): _____

_____

_____

About the Author

JoAnna Nicholson is President of Color 1 Associates, Inc., International Image & Style Consultants. As a founder of the image industry, she is a recipient of the prestigious Image Industry Council International (IICI) Award of Excellence and the IMMIE Award for Commitment, and has been a dynamic force in the industry for 25 years.

JoAnna, the author of four books, trains image and style consultants all over the world and she has been an instructor and director of self-improvement in a fashion merchandising college, is a former model, and co-founder of an interior design studio. Her home, which she designed using the Color 1 Concept, has been featured in *Architectural Digest* and *Italian Architectural Digest*.

Lecturing internationally and nationally on color, style, wardrobe, makeup, and interior design, JoAnna has conducted seminars at the invitation of the American Embassy in Paris. Her television and radio appearances include the *Montel Williams Show* and the *Larry King Show*.

JoAnna's other books, *How to Be Sexy Without Looking Sleazy, 110 Mistakes Working Women Make & How to Avoid Them: Dressing Smart in the '90s,* and *Color Wonderful,* have been featured in *Bazaar, Cosmopolitan, Redbook, Complete Woman, Woman's Own* and over 100 newspapers.

Business & Career Resources

Contact Impact Publications for a free annotated listing of resources or visit the World Wide Web for a complete listing of resources: www.impactpublications.com. The following books are available directly from Impact Publications. Complete the following form or list the titles, include postage (see formula at the end), enclose payment, and send your order to:

IMPACT PUBLICATIONS
9104-N Manassas Drive
Manassas Park, VA 20111-5211
Tel 1-800/361-1055, 703/361-7300, or Fax 703/335-9486
Quick and easy online ordering: *www.impactpublications.com*

Qty.	Titles	Price	Total
IMAGE AND ETIQUETTE			
_____	Business Etiquette and Professionalism	10.95	_____
_____	Dressing Smart in the New Millennium	13.95	_____
_____	Executive Etiquette in the New Workplace	14.95	_____
_____	First Five Minutes	14.95	_____
_____	John Malloy's Dress for Success (For Men)	13.99	_____
_____	Lions Don't Need to Roar	10.99	_____
_____	New Professional Image	12.95	_____
_____	New Women's Dress for Success	12.99	_____
_____	Red Socks Don't Work	14.95	_____
_____	Winning Image	17.95	_____
_____	You've Only Got 3 Seconds	22.95	_____
BUSINESS ESSENTIALS			
_____	101 Mistakes Employers Make and How to Avoid Them	14.95	_____
_____	101 Secrets of Highly Effective Speakers	14.95	_____
_____	The Best 100 Web Sites for HR Professionals	12.95	_____
_____	Employer's Guide to Recruiting on the Internet	24.95	_____
_____	Recruit and Retain the Best	14.95	_____
_____	Take This Job and Thrive	14.95	_____
INTERNET JOB SEARCH/HIRING			
_____	Career Exploration On the Internet	15.95	_____
_____	Electronic Resumes	19.95	_____
_____	Employer's Guide to Recruiting on the Internet	24.95	_____
_____	Guide to Internet Job Search.	14.95	_____
_____	Heart & Soul Internet Job Search	16.95	_____
_____	How to Get Your Dream Job Using the Web	29.99	_____
_____	Internet Jobs Kit	149.95	_____
_____	Internet Resumes	14.95	_____
_____	Job Searching Online for Dummies	24.99	_____
_____	Resumes in Cyberspace	14.95	_____

ALTERNATIVE JOBS & EMPLOYERS

_____	100 Best Careers for the 21st Century	15.95	_____
_____	100 Great Jobs and How To Get Them	17.95	_____
_____	101 Careers	16.95	_____
_____	150 Best Companies for Liberal Arts Graduates	15.95	_____
_____	50 Coolest Jobs in Sports	15.95	_____
_____	Adams Job Almanac 2000	16.95	_____
_____	American Almanac of Jobs and Salaries	20.00	_____
_____	Back Door Guide to Short-Term Job Adventures	19.95	_____
_____	Best Jobs for the 21st Century	19.95	_____
_____	Breaking & Entering	17.95	_____
_____	Careers in Computers	17.95	_____
_____	Careers in Health Care	17.95	_____
_____	Careers in High Tech	17.95	_____
_____	Career Smarts	12.95	_____
_____	Cool Careers for Dummies	16.95	_____
_____	Cybercareers	24.95	_____
_____	Directory of Executive Recruiters	44.95	_____
_____	Flight Attendant Job Finder	16.95	_____
_____	Great Jobs Ahead	11.95	_____
_____	Health Care Job Explosion!	17.95	_____
_____	Hidden Job Market 2000	18.95	_____
_____	High-Skill, High-Wage Jobs	19.95	_____
_____	JobBank Guide to Computer and High-Tech Companies	16.95	_____
_____	JobSmarts Guide to Top 50 Jobs	15.00	_____
_____	Liberal Arts Jobs	14.95	_____
_____	Media Companies 2000	18.95	_____
_____	Quantum Companies II	26.95	_____
_____	Sunshine Jobs	16.95	_____
_____	Take It From Me	12.00	_____
_____	Top 100	19.95	_____
_____	Top 2,500 Employers 2000	18.95	_____
_____	Trends 2000	14.99	_____
_____	What Employers Really Want	14.95	_____
_____	Working in TV News	12.95	_____
_____	Workstyles to Fit Your Lifestyle	11.95	_____
_____	You Can't Play the Game If You Don't Know the Rules	14.95	_____

RECRUITERS/EMPLOYERS

_____	Adams Executive Recruiters Almanac	16.95	_____
_____	Directory of Executive Recruiters	44.95	_____
_____	Employer's Guide to Recruiting on the Internet	24.95	_____

JOB STRATEGIES AND TACTICS

_____	101 Ways to Power Up Your Job Search	12.95	_____
_____	110 Big Mistakes Job Hunters	19.95	_____
_____	24 Hours to Your Next Job, Raise, or Promotion	10.95	_____
_____	Better Book for Getting Hired	11.95	_____
_____	Career Bounce-Back	14.95	_____
_____	Career Chase	17.95	_____
_____	Career Fitness	19.95	_____
_____	Career Intelligence	15.95	_____
_____	Career Starter	10.95	_____
_____	Coming Alive From 9 to 5	18.95	_____
_____	Complete Idiot's Guide to Changing Careers	17.95	_____
_____	Executive Job Search Strategies	16.95	_____
_____	First Job Hunt Survival Guide	11.95	_____
_____	Five Secrets to Finding a Job	12.95	_____
_____	Get a Job You Love!	19.95	_____
_____	Get It Together By 30	14.95	_____
_____	Get the Job You Want Series	37.95	_____
_____	Get Ahead! Stay Ahead!	12.95	_____
_____	Getting from Fired to Hired	14.95	_____

_____	Great Jobs for Liberal Arts Majors	11.95 _____
_____	How to Get a Job in 90 Days or Less	12.95 _____
_____	How to Get Interviews from Classified Job Ads	14.95 _____
_____	How to Succeed Without a Career Path	13.95 _____
_____	How to Get the Job You Really Want	9.95 _____
_____	How to Make Use of a Useless Degree	13.00 _____
_____	Is It Too Late To Run Away and Join the Circus?	14.95 _____
_____	Job Hunting in the 21st Century	17.95 _____
_____	Job Hunting for the Utterly Confused	14.95 _____
_____	Job Hunting Made Easy	12.95 _____
_____	Job Search: The Total System	14.95 _____
_____	Job Search Organizer	12.95 _____
_____	Job Search Time Manager	14.95 _____
_____	JobShift	13.00 _____
_____	JobSmart	12.00 _____
_____	Kiplinger's Survive and Profit From a Mid-Career Change	12.95 _____
_____	Knock 'Em Dead	12.95 _____
_____	Me, Myself, and I, Inc.	17.95 _____
_____	New Rights of Passage	29.95 _____
_____	No One Is Unemployable	29.95 _____
_____	Not Just Another Job	12.00 _____
_____	Part-Time Careers	10.95 _____
_____	Perfect Job Search	12.95 _____
_____	Princeton Review Guide to Your Career	20.00 _____
_____	Perfect Pitch	13.99 _____
_____	Portable Executive	12.00 _____
_____	Professional's Job Finder	18.95 _____
_____	Reinventing Your Career	9.99 _____
_____	Resumes Don't Get Jobs	10.95 _____
_____	Right Fit	14.95 _____
_____	Right Place at the Right Time	11.95 _____
_____	Second Careers	14.95 _____
_____	Secrets from the Search Firm Files	24.95 _____
_____	So What If I'm 50	12.95 _____
_____	Staying in Demand	12.95 _____
_____	Strategic Job Jumping	13.00 _____
_____	SuccessAbilities	14.95 _____
_____	Take Yourself to the Top	13.99 _____
_____	Temping: The Insiders Guide	14.95 _____
_____	Top 10 Career Strategies for the Year 2000 & Beyond	12.00 _____
_____	Top 10 Fears of Job Seekers	12.00 _____
_____	Ultimate Job Search Survival	14.95 _____
_____	VGMs Career Checklist	9.95 _____
_____	Welcome to the Real World	13.00 _____
_____	What Do I Say Next?	20.00 _____
_____	What Employers Really Want	14.95 _____
_____	When Do I Start	11.95 _____
_____	Who Says There Are No Jobs Out There	12.95 _____
_____	Work Happy Live Healthy	14.95 _____
_____	Work This Way	14.95 _____

ATTITUDE & MOTIVATION

_____	100 Ways to Motivate Yourself	15.99 _____
_____	Attitude Is Everything	14.99 _____
_____	Change Your Attitude	15.99 _____
_____	Reinventing Yourself	18.99 _____

INSPIRATION & EMPOWERMENT

_____	10 Stupid Things Men Do to Mess Up Their Lives	13.00 _____
_____	10 Stupid Things Women Do	13.00 _____
_____	101 Great Resumes	9.99 _____
_____	101 Simple Ways to Be Good to Yourself	12.95 _____
_____	Awaken the Giant Within	12.00 _____

_____	Beating Job Burnout	12.95 _____
_____	Big Things Happen When You Do the Little Things Right	15.00 _____
_____	Career Busters	10.95 _____
_____	Chicken Soup for the Soul Series	87.95 _____
_____	Do What You Love, the Money Will Follow	11.95 _____
_____	Doing It All Isn't Everything	19.95 _____
_____	Doing Work You Love	14.95 _____
_____	Emotional Intelligence	13.95 _____
_____	First Things First	23.00 _____
_____	Get What You Deserve	23.00 _____
_____	Getting Unstuck	11.99 _____
_____	If It's Going To Be, It's Up To Me	22.00 _____
_____	If Life Is A Game, These Are the Rules	15.00 _____
_____	In Search of Values	8.99 _____
_____	Job/Family Challenge: A 9-5 Guide	12.95 _____
_____	Kick In the Seat of the Pants	11.95 _____
_____	Kiplinger's Taming the Paper Tiger	11.95 _____
_____	Life Skills	17.95 _____
_____	Love Your Work and SuccessWill Follow	12.95 _____
_____	Path, The	14.95 _____
_____	Personal Job Power	12.95 _____
_____	Power of Purpose	20.00 _____
_____	Seven Habits of Highly Effective People	14.00 _____
_____	Softpower	10.95 _____
_____	Stop Postponing the Rest of Your Life	9.95 _____
_____	Suvivor Personality	12.00 _____
_____	To Build the Life You Want, Create the Work You Love	10.95 _____
_____	Unlimited Power	12.00 _____
_____	Wake-Up Calls	18.95 _____
_____	Your Signature Path	24.95 _____

TESTING AND ASSESSMENT

_____	Career Counselor's Tool Kit	45.00 _____
_____	Career Discovery Project	12.95 _____
_____	Career Exploration Inventory	29.95 _____
_____	Career Satisfaction and Success	14.95 _____
_____	Career Tests	12.95 _____
_____	Crystal-Barkley Guideto Taking Charge of Your Career	9.95 _____
_____	Dictionary of Holland Occupational Codes	45.00 _____
_____	Discover the Best Jobs For You	14.95 _____
_____	Discover What You're Best At	12.00 _____
_____	Gifts Differing	14.95 _____
_____	Have You Got What It Takes?	12.95 _____
_____	How to Find the Work You Love	10.95 _____
_____	Making Vocational Choices	29.95 _____
_____	New Quick Job Hunting Map	4.95 _____
_____	P.I.E. Method for Career Success	14.95 _____
_____	Putting Your Talent to Work	12.95 _____
_____	Real People, Real Jobs	15.95 _____
_____	Starting Out, Starting Over	14.95 _____
_____	Test Your IQ	6.95 _____
_____	Three Boxes of Life	18.95 _____
_____	Type Talk	11.95 _____
_____	WORKTypes	12.99 _____
_____	You and Co., Inc.	22.00 _____
_____	Your Hidden Assets	19.95 _____

RESUMES & LETTERS

_____	$110,000 Resume	16.95 _____
_____	100 Winning Resumes for $100,000+ Jobs	24.95 _____
_____	101 Best Resumes	10.95 _____
_____	101 More Best Resumes	11.95 _____
_____	101 Quick Tips for a Dynamite Resume	13.95 _____

_____	1500+ Key Words for 100,000+	14.95	_____
_____	175 High-Impact Resumes	10.95	_____
_____	Adams Resume Almanac/Disk	19.95	_____
_____	America's Top Resumes for America's Top Jobs	19.95	_____
_____	Asher's Bible of Exec.utive Resumes	29.95	_____
_____	Best Resumes for $75,000+ Executive Jobs	14.95	_____
_____	Best Resumes for Attorneys	16.95	_____
_____	Better Resumes in Three Easy Steps	12.95	_____
_____	Blue Collar and Beyond	8.95	_____
_____	Blue Collar Resumes	11.99	_____
_____	Building a Great Resume	15.00	_____
_____	Cyberspace Resume Kit	16.95	_____
_____	Damn Good Resume Guide	7.95	_____
_____	Dynamite Resumes	14.95	_____
_____	Edge Resume and Job Search Strategy	23.95	_____
_____	Electronic Resumes and Onlline Networking	13.99	_____
_____	Encyclopedia of Job-Winning Resumes	16.95	_____
_____	Gallery of Best Resumes	16.95	_____
_____	Heart & Soul Resumes	15.95	_____
_____	High Impact Resumes and Letters	19.95	_____
_____	Just Resumes	11.95	_____
_____	New Perfect Resume	10.95	_____
_____	Overnight Resume	12.95	_____
_____	Portfolio Power	14.95	_____
_____	Power Resumes	14.95	_____
_____	Prof. Resumes/Executives, Managers, & Other Administrators	19.95	_____
_____	Professional "Resumes For..." Career Series	213.95	_____
_____	Quick Resume and Cover Letter Book	12.95	_____
_____	Ready-To-Go Resumes	29.95	_____
_____	Resume Catalog	15.95	_____
_____	Resume Magic	18.95	_____
_____	Resume Power	12.95	_____
_____	Resume Pro	24.95	_____
_____	Resume Shortcuts	14.95	_____
_____	Resume Writing Made Easy	11.95	_____
_____	Resumes for the Over-50 Job Hunter	14.95	_____
_____	Resumes for Re-Entry	10.95	_____
_____	Resume Winners from the Pros	17.95	_____
_____	Resumes for Dummies	12.99	_____
_____	Resumes for the Health Care Professional	14.95	_____
_____	Resumes That Knock 'Em Dead	10.95	_____
_____	Resumes That Will Get You the Job You Want	12.99	_____
_____	Savvy Resume Writer	10.95	_____
_____	Sure-Hire Resumes	14.95	_____
_____	Winning Resumes	10.95	_____

COVER LETTERS

_____	101 Best Cover Letters	11.95	_____
_____	175 High-Impact Cover Letters	10.95	_____
_____	200 Letters for Job Hunters	19.95	_____
_____	201 Winning Cover Letters for the $100,000+ Jobs	24.95	_____
_____	201 Dynamite Job Search Letters	19.95	_____
_____	201 Killer Cover Letters	16.95	_____
_____	Complete Idiot's Guide to the Perfect Cover Letters	14.95	_____
_____	Cover Letters for Dummies	12.99	_____
_____	Cover Letters that Knock 'Em Dead	10.95	_____
_____	Dynamite Cover Letters	14.95	_____
_____	Gallery of Best Cover Letters	18.95	_____
_____	Haldane's Best Cover Letters for Professionals	15.95	_____
_____	Perfect Cover Letter	10.95	_____
_____	Winning Cover Letters	10.95	_____

INTERVIEWING: JOBSEEKERS

_____	101 Dynamite Answers to Interview Questions	12.95 _____
_____	101 Dynamite Questions to Ask at Your Job Interview	14.95 _____
_____	101 Tough Interview Questions. . .	14.95 _____
_____	111 Dynamite Ways to Ace Your Job Interview	13.95 _____
_____	Haldane's Best Answers to Tough Interview Questions	15.95 _____
_____	Information Interviewing	10.95 _____
_____	Interview for Success	15.95 _____
_____	Job Interviews for Dummies	12.99 _____
_____	Savvy Interviewer	10.95 _____

NETWORKING

_____	Dig Your Well Before You're Thirsty	24.95 _____
_____	Dynamite Networking for Dynamite Jobs	15.95 _____
_____	Dynamite Tele-Search	12.95 _____
_____	Golden Rule of Schmoozing	12.95 _____
_____	Great Connections	11.95 _____
_____	How to Work a Room	11.99 _____
_____	Network Your Way to Success	19.95 _____
_____	Networking for Everyone	16.95 _____
_____	Power Networking	14.95 _____
_____	Power Schmoozing	12.95 _____
_____	Power To Get In	24.95 _____

SALARY NEGOTIATIONS

_____	Dynamite Salary Negotiations	15.95 _____
_____	Get a Raise in 7 Days	14.95 _____
_____	Get More Money on Your Next Job	14.95 _____
_____	Negotiate Your Job Offer	14.95 _____

☞ **SUBTOTAL** $ _____

☞ Virginia residents add 4½% sales tax) _____

☞ Shipping/handling, Continental U.S., $5.00 +   _____ $5.00
plus following percentages when **SUBTOTAL** is:

- ❑ $30-$100—multiply SUBTOTAL by 8%   _____
- ❑ $100-$999—multiply SUBTOTAL by 7%   _____
- ❑ $1,000-$4,999—multiply SUBTOTAL by 6%   _____
- ❑ Over $5,000—multiply SUBTOTAL by 5%   _____

☞ ❑ If shipped outside Continental US, add another 5%   _____

☞ **TOTAL ENCLOSED** $_____

SHIP TO: (street address only for UPS or RPS delivery)

Name _____

Address _____

_____

_____

Telephone _____

I enclose ❑ Check ❑ Money Order in the amount of: $ _____

Charge $_____ to ❑ Visa ❑ MC ❑ AmEx

Card #_____ Exp: _____ / _____

Signature _____

Discover Hundreds of Additional Resources on the World Wide Web!

Looking for the newest and best books, directories, newsletters, wall charts, training programs, videos, computer software, and kits to help you land a job, negotiate a higher salary, or start your own business? Want to learn the most effective way to find a job in Asia or relocate to San Francisco? Are you curious about how to find a job 24 hours a day using the Internet or about what you'll be doing five years from now? Are you trying to keep up-to-date on the latest career resources, but are not able to find the latest catalogs, brochures, or newsletters on today's "best of the best" resources?

Welcome to the first virtual career bookstore on the Internet. Now you're only a click away with Impact Publications' electronic solution to the resource challenge. Visit this rich site to quickly discover everything you ever wanted to know about finding jobs, changing careers, and starting your own business—including many useful resources that are difficult to find in local bookstores and libraries. The site also includes what's new and hot, tips for job search success, and monthly specials. Check it out today!

www.impactpublications.com